Dennis Gibbs

The Gospel Life

All rights reserved. No part of this publication may be repro-
duced, stored in a retrieval system or transmited in any form or
by any means, electronic, mechanical, photocopying, recording
or otherwise without the prior permision of the publisher or in
accordance with the provisions of the Copyright, Designs and
Patents Act 1988 or under the terms of any licence permitting
limited copying issued by the Copyright Licensing Angency.

Published by: Sacred Journey Publishing

Edited by: Alysha Kawamoto

Cover Design by: Carrie Voris

A CIP record for this book is acailable from the Library of Con-
gress Cataloging-in-Publication Data

ISBN-10: 1-7379683-0-6

ISBN-13: 978-1-7379683-0-6

Printed and bound by Sacred Journey Publications

Dennis Gibbs

THE GOSPEL LIFE

Sacred Journey Publications

SECOND EDITION

THE GOSPEL LIFE

Dennis Gibbs

To all my friends living behind the wall.

Table of Contents

Introduction

One day, I was visiting with an inmate in the L.A. County jail, as I have done for many years. It was a good visit, with nothing out of the ordinary, but as I was leaving, my friend asked me, "Do you have some of your writing for me today?" He was referring to the short essays on life and Gospel interpretations that I had begun to write and distribute. He went on to explain how much he appreciated my take on things, and that he had saved each one. Later, my friend Mary in CRDF (the women's jail facility), would refer to these essays as "one-pagers."

For a long time, beginning a few years into my sobriety and recovery, friends have suggested that I tell my story in book form. At first, I was not convinced. The question that I could not answer was: why write a book, when I could continue to share my experience, strength, and hope with others in the oral tradition done so beautifully in the 12-Step recovery programs and fellowships? To write a book just so I could say that I was a published author wasn't a good enough reason. But I did start writing.

Over the next several years, the inspiration for one-pagers kept coming and I kept writing them. Then came that visitation in the jail, when my friend asked about my writing and told me why it was important to him. In that moment, I realized why I would write a book. It would be for him, and for so many others like him.

The first book, *Oblivion: Grace in Exile with a Monk Behind Bars*, was published in 2019. It was partly auto-biography and partly the stories of our friends relegated to living in exile. I wanted to bring a voice to those who had been rendered silent. I wanted to tell the world what I had learned from these friends about grace, resilience, and dignity. The stories are beautiful because the people in them are. The stories are powerful because they strike at the heart of the human condition with truth and authenticity.

The Gospel Life seems to be a natural progression. Many of the short essays (some taken from one-pagers I have previously written and others from brand-new writings) are framed around the Gospel stories and teachings of Jesus. Others are taken from ordinary life experiences. There is original poetry and photography as well. Through it all, I hope that you will discover that our very lives are sacred texts; that we ourselves are the living Gospel.

We can all learn much from the wisdom and literature of the many spiritual traditions of the world. We can also learn from our relationships with one another. Ultimately, the truth we seek is not hidden in some far-off secret place. It sits at the center of our being, just waiting to be discovered when we share our lives together with loving intention. It is then that we begin to see God in each other and experience the "Good News."

This is the Gospel life.

The Illusion of Separateness and a Call to Unity

Lectio Divina, which is Latin for "Divine Reading," is an ancient Christian practice of reading scripture in a contemplative way. The process begins with reading through a piece of sacred text and waiting for a single word, sentence, or phrase to offer itself for deeper reflection. Once, in our group Lectio Divina practice at the monastery, the word from scripture that stood out for me was "separate." I felt that God was asking me to reflect on that word in all its forms: *separate, separation, separateness, separating.*

The idea of separation feels like a timely consideration when there seems to be so many temptations to think in terms of being separate from, different from, or even in opposition with one another. I have often said, and believe to be true, that any perception that we are somehow separate from each other is an illusion.

In so many ways, we are prone to falling into the trap of separateness – the "us" or "them" dualistic mindset – but that is not the nature of God and how we were created.

The nature of God, so beautifully expressed in the life of Jesus, was all about community. Jesus was about *unifying consciousness*, which is very different from the *illusion of separateness*. The illusion of separateness fosters division, competition, and tribal mentality, whereas a unifying consciousness fosters unity, compassion, and communal sharing. The illusion of separateness operates from scarcity and finite fear. A unifying consciousness operates from a sense of abundance and infinite love.

A friend of mine says, "Relationship is primary; everything else is secondary." I feel there is great wisdom in those words. However, we seem to find almost interminable ways to separate ourselves. We put up dividers that not only box in people, but also imprison our own hearts, in ways that disallow relational flourishing. We are created for community, yet in recent years we have, in many ways, been headed the opposite direction into the illusion of separateness. The time has come for us to take off the labels that divide us, and take on our identity as a community together in this thing called life.

What I love and appreciate about the life and teachings of Jesus is that he offers me a clear spiritual design for living that fosters community, compassion, mercy, justice, truth, and love. In a world that all too often wants to divide us, it is the teachings of Jesus as a model for life that guide me. His mandate is to care first for the sick, the poor, and most vulnerable of our human family, because no person should go without proper health care and protection. He instructs us to welcome the stranger, because we all have the right to seek a better life. Jesus is also clear about our pursuit of justice and true equality for all people because none of us are free until all of us are free. The gospel life calls for us to put away discrimination, marginalization, and disenfranchisement of any group, including our LGBTQ brothers and sisters. We are to care for one another regardless of national origin, denominational stripes, spiritual tradition, and political affiliation. We need desperately to put away the sins of racism, the death penalty, and all other violence against humanity, for they deteriorate our collective soul. Above all, Jesus asks us to love God with everything we have and to love one another at all costs. None of these things are about being "liberal" or "progressive;" they are about living the true gospel life as taught and modeled by Jesus.

These values are found in most every major spiritual tradition. This is a time for them to cast away any illusion of separateness, so we can together help guide a hurting world that is hungry for a sense of community and belonging. All religious and spiritual expressions have a tremendous opportunity to show the world what coming together for the common good of humanity can look like. The world needs us now; together, we can make the world a better place. As the Psalmist says: "Oh, how good and wonderful it is when people live in unity."

Bread for each Other

LUKE 24: 13-35

Skid Row in Los Angeles has roughly 10,000 homeless, poor, and marginally employed residents. The area, with its numerous street encampments, rescue missions, and single room occupancy hotels, has the dubious nickname of "the homeless capital of the nation." It is also the most policed area in the country. In the heart of it all is the Hospitality Kitchen, also known as the "Hippie Kitchen," one of the many programs run by the Catholic Worker program. The soup kitchen offers hot meals three days per week to thousands of our brothers and sisters in need, and also has a medical and dental clinic on-site with doctors and nurses volunteering their time on a continual rotating basis.

On the wall that faces 6th Street as you approach the Hospitality Kitchen, there is a large mural, beautifully painted and depicting the homeless community lining up for food. A closer look reveals that one of those people is Jesus himself, simply getting in line with the others. This powerful image serves as a reminder that God is in full solidarity with all of humanity and stands with the poorest among us. For me, this mural is an icon of the appearance stories that we hear each year during the time of Easter after Jesus' resurrection.

One of those stories tells of him joining two of his followers as they journeyed along the road to Emmaus. He came quietly into stride, as if it were the most natural thing in the world, and joined in the conversation. The disciples, however, did not realize it was him. It was only later, when he sat with them at the table in their home, that something familiar happened: he took the bread, blessed it, and gave it to them. It was in that moment that his friends remembered their last meal together in the upper room – the same words, the same blessing, the same undeniable sense of love and solidarity. In community, as companions, Jesus became known to them in the breaking of the bread.

The Latin root word for "companion" is *companis*, which means *"bread"* or *"loaf,"* or more literally, *"to be bread for one another."* We are all called to be companions along the way with each other. We are all called to be bread for each other and to nourish one another. On the sacred journey of life, we will meet many people along the way: people who are struggling, and people who help us when we stumble. The road to Emmaus winds through our city streets, the soup kitchens, jails and prisons; the hospitals and slums. It runs through the COVID isolation chambers and the salute of banging pots and pans for hospital workers as they return home from the front lines of the pandemic. It takes us through the bloodshed of Palestine and the poverty of Haiti, and on the road of exile with our Syrian sisters and brothers. It runs along the hillsides and ocean beaches and onto 6th & Gladys in skid row. All along the way, we are called to be bread for each other. We are called to nourish one another with food and dignity.

When we encounter one another on this Communion Road and respond to the needs and hopes of others, we are given the opportunity to engage in real, positive change in the lives of our global community. In the process, we are transformed. Through it all, God is with us, and it is in these communal acts of love and mercy that the Reality of God comes into focus. It is then that, as Christians, we know Jesus in the breaking of the bread – in the giving of ourselves to each other. It is then that the Divine Reality becomes real for all people of every tradition in their own understanding. This bread of life – the *companis* – is baked with love, a love that is big enough for all people everywhere, regardless of spiritual tradition, national origin, life orientation, denominational stripes, or political affiliation. The Road to Emmaus is for all people and will take us to the one truth that we are all in this together.

On this road, we will never look into the eyes of anyone that God does not love. On this road, God becomes one of us. On this road, we become one with God, because we all share the one bread of our collective soul dipped in Divine Love.

How have you been a companion for others? Who has been your companion? What have you learned by being in companionship?

Second Chances

LUKE 24: 13-35

I think most of us can relate to the need to sometimes re-calibrate – to get back to basics – and to return to a sense of the core truth of who we are when things start spinning out of control. It is good to step out of the chaos and reclaim ourselves. My 12-Step recovery work surely helps return me to my center; sometimes I just need silence in nature, or time with an art project in the monk's shed at the monastery. I might take time to do some writing or meditation. These things help to return me to my center and quiet the disturbance within.

One of my favorite Gospel stories is about Jesus's appearing to the disciples on the beach after the resurrection. Peter in particular was lost in shame and guilt after the dizzying events of Jesus's arrest, conviction, sentencing, and execution. He had abandoned his Lord, even denied knowing his dearest friend when it counted most. He had been knocked so far off the beam of who he thought he was that now that he didn't know quite what to do or where to turn. So what did he do? He went fishing.

Peter was a fisherman. That is what he knew. Amid the chaos, that is where he found his center. On this day when Peter was swimming in confusion and heartbreak at the loss of his truest friend, he needed some time to sort things out. So, he went fishing.

It was on these same shores that Jesus first met him, and that is where Jesus found him again. In this lovely moment between a broken man and his Messiah, they sat next to the fire and ate breakfast. One cannot help but wonder if Peter was thinking of another fire – the one he warmed himself next to as Jesus was imprisoned, while he himself remained warm and safe. Now, the quiet between the two as they sat by the fire was the hospitality of love in its most fundamental state.

Jesus broke the silence. That is how God is, always gracious in helping us move beyond our limitations. He called Peter by the name he had before they knew each other: "Simon, son of John." Referring to Peter in this way took them back to an earlier time – a new start, a second chance. Jesus knew there was no value in re-hashing the details that had caused Peter's guilt and shame. Instead, he restored Peter in love, not once, not twice, but three times, asking the ever-deepening question, "Peter, do you love me?" Peter, who before denied Jesus three times, was now three times restored in love.

Like Peter, most of us are so ordinarily human, so simple and yet so complex. That is how it is with the primary characters in the Gospel narratives. They are composites of ourselves. That is why we connect with them, and Peter is no exception. The next time we feel a little lost in our faith journey – when we feel as though we have somehow let God down, that we need to make better sense of things and re-gain perspective – we can remember this story of how God comes to us in love, meeting us where we are, cooking breakfast on the beach, and offering us yet another chance.

God's love comes to us
on the beaches of our life
with a second chance

Dining with Carl

HEBREWS 13:2

Before I took monastic vows and entered the monastery, I lived in Burbank. There was a small locally-owned diner that I used to go to occasionally, the kind of place where most of the customers were known by name. But one evening, there was a stranger. I would learn later that his name was Carl.

Carl sat at one of the tables with his backpack, as though he carried his whole life with him. I guess that is true for all of us in a way – we all carry the invisible backpacks of our lives with us. He had the look of one who has been traveling under the sun for a long time. A single cup of coffee sat in front of him. Still, I sensed both a heaviness and pleasantness about him.

The energy in the small diner space felt more like hostility than hospitality. People cast suspicious glances in Carl's direction as if he were some sort of bother or intrusion, of which I could see no evidence; he was quietly sitting in his booth and keeping to himself. Every few minutes the waitress would come by with the coffee pot, and with a certain sophistication, he would sip from his cup before offering it politely for refill. She would refill the cup and walk away, turning her face away from him and rolling her eyes in disapproval.

After a while, Carl got up from his seat and went into the bathroom. That was when people stopped being so reserved in their impoliteness. With each passing minute that Carl was still in the men's room, the mood of those working in the diner grew increasingly impatient. One of the waitresses knocked loudly on the door and called for Carl to come out. A muffled response came from inside.

After another moment or two, Carl appeared and quietly made his way to his seat. His dignity defied the unwarranted hostility of those around him. The waitress followed him, now asking – not in any kind or respectful way – that he leave the diner, saying he was bothering the customers. It seemed to me that the only bother was that Carl appeared different. And he *was* different – unlike those around him, he remained polite, and respectful, and dignified through it all.

When the waitress raised her voice because Carl apparently wasn't moving fast enough for her, I couldn't take it any longer. Leaving my meal, I walked over to Carl, and asked him if he would like to join me at my table. He looked at me – sizing me up, I suppose – but then, looking me squarely in the eye, said "yes."

I looked at the waitress and said: "He's with me." Much to her chagrin, we moved to our booth. Carl ordered a meal and we began to talk.

I learned that Carl was from Seattle. He told me about his wife and how he had not been able to regain his footing after her untimely death. He told me about his daughter and two grandchildren who were living in Oregon. That was where he was heading: home, to family. The waitress, who had been nice enough to me before, lost her cheerful disposition as she served Carl his meal. She gave me a look that said, "You sure have a lot of nerve." She was right.

In the meantime, Carl was a perfect gentleman, always saying, "thank you" and "please" and expressing his appreciation. He was the kindest and most respectful person in the room. I felt like I was dining with Jesus.

Afterward, I asked if I could drive him anywhere, and Carl said he would love to go to the library. As we headed out, I left a tip for the waitress. If Carl could have so much grace, I could at least try. And there were the words of Jesus ringing in my ears: *"To love those who persecute you, this is the real test of love."* I added another dollar to the tip.

Once at the library, Carl said he had something he wanted to show me. He led me to one of the computers, logged in to his email, and began showing me photographs of his daughter Ruth and his two grandchildren Chloe and Andrew. His face lit up with excitement and his eyes sparkled with love and pride as he told me about his family. After a while, I took my eyes off the clock and allowed myself to be gathered into this experience of real hospitality.

Later, we sat exchanging stories on the bench of the Greyhound bus terminal waiting for his ride to Oregon. My last vision of him was him climbing aboard with my phone number in his pocket and waving goodbye. I never heard from Carl again. I think of him often. Even though we had only two or three hours together, we had friendship, and I am grateful we met.

That day, I learned from him that hospitality isn't only about opening ourselves to others, it is also about allowing hearts to be reached and touched by others. He taught me

23

that humility is about being honest with yourself about who you are, and when you hold that kind of truth for yourself, no one can define you, not even a waitress in a diner.

Hospitality in community is more than a simple handshake or a "Hello, my name is..." sticker. It is seeing and accepting people for who they are. It is allowing ourselves to experience how our community can be enriched by others' presence, instead of expecting them to change to fit our established mold.

Never Give up on Goodness

MATTHEW 18:15-17

There is a story in the New Testament Gospel of Matthew about how we should reconcile when someone has harmed us or others. In it, Jesus advises that we should make repeated attempts to heal the divide. He says that if the initial attempt at reconciliation fails, then we should involve others and try again, and again, and yet again. In no way should this be interpreted as license to gang up on someone. It is not about pressuring the person to see things our way. It is simply about not giving up. Jesus did not mean that we should keep coming at a person again and again until we get what *we* want. Instead, we should keep coming to them until God gets what God wants.

Once Peter asked Jesus, *"How many times must I forgive?"* Jesus answered, *"Seventy times seven."* The number seven was considered to represent fullness or completeness, and this directive from Jesus says basically that our forgiveness should be endless. It is a statement about hope in the goodness in each of us, even in the one who has harmed us. It is about never giving up on ourselves because God will never give up on us.

The vision of PRISM Restorative Justice is this: *A world in which all people are restored to wholeness through the love of God.* Restorative justice has its roots in New Zealand and is modeled by the indigenous Maori People. It is a process that involves calling the community together when the fabric of their common life has been torn by a hurtful act. The process involves those on both sides of the offense – the offender and the offended – as well as representatives of the entire community. They believe that when one member of the community is hurt, they are all hurt. When one has gone astray, they have all gone astray, and they are all responsible for each other in the process of healing. The goal is always for the person who has offended to be restored back into the community.

An essential part of the process is to first have those involved gather in a sacred circle around the person in who has committed the offense and speak out loud about the positive aspects of their character and personality. One by one, they acknowledge what they know of the goodness of the person. This is the starting point.

How different things might be if we could somehow look for the goodness of a person as our starting point and to never give up – to be relentless in our pursuit of their best nature. Think of how much easier it would be to have difficult conversations with people if we began by acknowledging their goodness, if we began by speaking their truth back to them: the truth that they are a child of God and they are beloved by God. In doing so, we just might hear the echo of our own truth speaking back to us. This is what Jesus calls us to do. He asks that we never, ever give up on each other and the good that lives within each of us.

In so many ways, we have forgotten that we belong to one another. I pray that we will truly know in our hearts that we are indeed one people, one family of God, called to love one another as Christ loves us. As my friend Fr. Greg Boyle says: "There is no 'us' or 'them' – there is only us." There are no throwaway people. No one is beyond the grace and love of God. These are truths that become self-evident when we begin looking for, and never giving up on, the goodness in each other. If there is anything that we as followers of Jesus owe each other and the world, it is nothing other than the kind of relentless love that he modeled for us. It is a love that knows no bounds, no limits. It is a love that keeps coming at us again and again. It is a love that says that our pursuit of God is only outdone by God's pursuit of us.

God expects us to have the greatness of heart to hope in, and work for, the goodness within each of us, even those who hurt or disappoint us. That is also Paul's message about love: that it is the ultimate debt we owe one another. It is, in the final analysis, a love that simply refuses to give up on us, a love that is always with us, and a love that expects and deserves nothing less than our best. We are then led to the question of whether we are willing to give ourselves fully to the love that gives itself fully to us. How we answer that question can revolutionize how we see ourselves in relationship with God and one another.

Can you always look for the goodness in another person? How might it change your life? How does it affect your ability to accept your own goodness?

Letters Between Friends

back and forth they move
like tides pulled by the moon
letters between friends

Each year, I exchange hundreds of letters with my friends living behind the walls of prisons. This poem speaks to the give and take – the coming and going – of those letters. My friends on the other end have become my teachers and spiritual companions from whom I have learned so much about real life and spirituality. These are my true brothers and sisters.

Over the years, I have had deep and meaningful encounters with so many in jails and prisons. Our hearts break. Our spirits soar. We laugh and cry together. We drink from both the cup of tears and the cup of salvation. We hold each other with our hands in prayer, and in our hearts with love. We experience sadness and joy, despair and hope, and walk together from darkness into light. I have witnessed real conversion, and I have learned what that means in my own life. Through it all, we remind each other that we are never alone and that we are never forgotten. We remind each other that no one is beyond the grace and love of God.

Practice writing notes, letters, and cards, and sending them to friends and family. Consider this simple act of thoughtfulness as a spiritual practice.

The First Year

The first year of my sobriety was not easy. While many of the other newcomers to recovery around me were experiencing what we call "The Pink Cloud" effect of new sobriety, for me it was more like a perpetual severe weather warning with storm clouds and lightning off in the distance. The obsession to drink and use something – anything – stayed with me through that first year.

I was fortunate enough to be introduced to people in the recovery community that helped me get a solid foothold in my sobriety, none more helpful and influential than the man who became my sponsor and now, over decades, my great friend in life and even a father figure. These wisdom teachers taught me the value of the fundamentals of life in recovery: honesty, open-mindedness, and willingness. My sponsor introduced me to the fellowship of others striving to achieve and maintain a life in recovery. They required from me a commitment to a basic frame of daily living: meetings, working the Twelve Steps, reaching out to others, and participating in the fellowship of those who cheerfully walked the path of freedom from addiction. It was a great time of my life, even a joyful time. And through it all I still wanted to drink and use.

That is the paradox in which some like me find themselves in recovery: the exhilarating sense of having been rescued from a disastrous shipwreck of a life, yet anxious that the tiny life raft you are clinging to might spring a leak and you will drown. Thankfully, those around me gave me simple yet life-saving tools to cope with the seemingly interminable mental and physical craving for something I knew would kill me should I succumb to its wicked advances.

I'm not sure when exactly the obsession to use drugs and alcohol left me. One day it was just gone, like a fog that had quietly lifted to reveal a whole new world of possibilities. All the promises that we talk about in the program of recovery have since come true for me over the past two-plus decades that I have been walking this road of happy destiny. Still, I will never forget those early days of struggle and grace. It helped form who I would become as a man in recovery. Many other challenges have come my way since, but I can always look back on those early days to remind me that I have been tested and I have been found worthy of this better life.

One day at a time.

The Circle, the Fire, the Story

We gather the circle
We light the fire
We tell the story.

The elders and the young
The women and the men
We sit in the round
Facing one another
So that we can see truth.

We light the sacred fire
Warming ourselves
Our gaze fixed on the steady glow
In the center of our being
Together we are held
Illumined by the flame of love.

We share our story
In this safe and sacred space
Honoring each heart with our own
We speak and we are free
We listen and we are love
Breaking our silence, we are healed.

We gather the circle
We light the fire
We tell our story.

Love Actually

JOHN 13:31-35

What is love *actually?* And by that, I mean how is love actualized in our lives? What does it look like in our everyday living? How does Divine Love – the loving essence of God – become real and affecting, right here and right now?

I heard one time of a woman who worked downtown and had an office that overlooked a small parish church. The church had a lunch program for those in need, and two or three times a week she would look down from her office perch and see the line of people being served by the parish. She was not a Christian, but one day she decided to go down and check it out. That first day eventually turned into once per week, and she would work silently next to others cooking, serving, and cleaning up. No one tried to convert her. They simply welcomed her to join them in doing something good out of kindness for others. It wasn't easy work, but it was worthwhile and she always returned to her office with a clearer perspective and a good feeling.

After a few months, the woman decided to attend church on a Sunday, and she found herself in the pews with some of the same people from both sides of the serving line. Soon she became a regular and eventually asked to be baptized. She had come to realize the actuality of love through simple acts of kindness.

I suspect that if the woman's experience is anything like my own, she not only experienced love for others, but she also experienced the love of Jesus as seen in the faces of those she engaged with. Experiences like these are when we realize that the Divine nature of love moves beyond service to others, and into real kinship with one another.

Hadewijch, the Thirteenth century mystic and one of the best known of the Beguine movement – the first Christian women's movement centered in living love both mystically and apostolically – said that *"One must live love."* Sr. Greta Ronningen, whose master's thesis was on the Beguines and who now leads women's retreats on Beguine Spirituality, would say that living love is not conceptual or theoretical, but that we must roll up our shirt sleeves and get moving. We must immerse ourselves in kinship with others in order to experience what I would call the *holy exchange of gifts.* Jesus makes it clear how we are to follow him into this radical, unconditional love, intimate with the world, when he said:

I was hungry and you gave me food, I was thirsty and you gave me something to drink, I was a stranger and you welcomed me, I was naked and you gave me clothing, I was sick and you took care of me, I was in prison and you visited me.

Truly I tell you, just as you did it to one of the least of these who are members of my family, you did it to me."

Love cannot be done from a distance. Love is something actualized in close proximity with each other. We need to see each other, touch each other, and help each other in real ways, like the woman standing in the lunch line at the parish; like the Beguines who lived among the lepers; like one recovering addict/alcoholic helping another; like the giving and receiving of acts of kindness between our friends who are locked up. Opportunities to share the abundance of God's love with each other are plentiful.

In the Episcopal Church, our baptismal covenant calls for us to *"proclaim by word and example the Good News of God in Christ. To seek and serve Christ in all persons, loving our neighbors as ourselves, to strive for justice and peace among all people, and to respect the dignity of every human being."* What more needs be said?

I often anoint my brothers and sisters in the jails, and I ask them to anoint me too. Sometimes, when I anoint their hands, I will say *"These are the hands of God in the world; use them well. Use them for love. Live as Jesus lived and teach to others what he has taught us."* It always feels real – like the original program – when we are reminded that we are all in this together, with Jesus as our teacher and guide in love.

To love actually is to love one another as Christ has loved us. It is to understand that the love modeled for us by Jesus is not for some, but for all. It is to understand that there is no "us" or "them," but that there is only us. The holy exchange of gifts flows both ways. We bring Christ and we see Christ. We are all both student and teacher. And as a result, we begin to know love, a love that feels real and authentic. I offer you these words from a great spiritual teacher of our time:

> *"I believe that the practice of compassion and love – a genuine sense of sisterhood and brotherhood – is universal religion. It does not matter whether you are Buddhist or a Christian, Hindu, Muslim, or Jew, or whether you practice religion at all. What matters is the feeling of oneness with humankind."*

Those words from the Dalai Lama resonate with deep truth for me, and maybe they do for you too.

If we as Christians are to have integrity, authenticity and relevance, we must show the world a love that moves beyond borders and dividing lines. It's a movement of Christ's love into *all* the world. It is about inspiring the very best in people. It is about loving and respecting the dignity of others in such a way that all people – regardless of religious tradition or denominational stripes – can claim and honor their own lives because of our presence, not in spite of it. Because of who we are and how we love, those around us can become more fully who they are and be inspired to love, and then we are one step closer to living into God's vision in which all people are restored to God in love. We are one step closer to realizing the Kingdom of heaven here on earth.

The twentieth century Trappist monk, activist, and writer Thomas Merton said: *"Love is my true identity. Selflessness is my true self. Love is my true character. Love is my name."*

Let's actually love each other in real, hands-on, no-strings-attached ways, with our touch, with our eyes, with a listening heart. Let's touch the world with what John of the Cross describes as the *living flame of love.* Abandon yourself to God and God's love. And remember that your hands are the hands of God in the world, so use them well. Live as Jesus lived, and teach to others what he has taught us. That is love, actually.

What does it mean for you to love?

How is love actualized in your life, and what does it look like?

Prodigal Love
JOHN 13:31-35

Many of us have had, or will have, times in our lives when we feel lost; when we feel separated from our truest self, from others, or even from God. I think that is why the Parable of the Two Sons – commonly known as "The Parable of the Prodigal Son" – is so well-known and related to by so many. It speaks to us because it is a story of redemption and hope.

As the story goes, the young son – out of greed, impatience, and a hunger for the world – insisted that his father give him his inheritance in advance, in a sense saying that he couldn't wait for his father to die. His father's response was surprising: He granted the request, giving him the money and sending him on his way. The young son then went off and squandered all of the money on wild living until he ended up destitute and friendless, a living epitome of deep separation, loneliness and despair.

To be starved of family, community, the human touch – to be starved of a sense that we are connected to the greater human family and to feel as though no one cares about us and loves us – this is a hunger that deteriorates the human soul. When the young son arrived at such a state, he did what most would hope to do: he turned toward home, to his family, to God. In that moment of clarity, he crafted his confession in hope that it would help him get back under his father's roof, and headed towards the only real home he had ever known. What happened next, when he got close enough to see his father's property in the distance, is what makes this story so special. It is what makes this a prodigal story.

While he was still a long way off, his father, who had been watching for him all along, ran out toward his son and pulled him close, before he could utter even a single word he had prepared. Imagine the moment and what it was like when they reached one another: the father out of breath, trembling with joy, weeping with love, and clutching his son like he will never let him go again; the son, his knees giving out, falling into his father, his shame burying his face into his father's chest. And then the father does the only thing there is to do. He gently lifts his boy's face to his, and kisses him.

What follows is a huge celebration in honor of his young son's return. This is extravagant, reckless, prodigal love pouring out from a father to his child. This is a story that says we can never stray so far away that we wouldn't be welcomed home with the embrace of grace. This is a story that says that our pursuit of God is only outdone by God's pursuit of us. This is the nature of prodigal love.

The coming home of the younger son and the celebration in response to his return would have been a good enough ending, but there is more to the story. Remember, this is a story about *two* sons.

The older son is not so quick to celebrate his brother's return. And who can blame him? It is one thing to welcome home the wayward troublemaker without so much as a heart-to-heart talk about things – without a form of penance to sort things out – but the older brother is still out in the fields working his tail off when the party starts. Where is the moral lesson in that? What about being accountable for your actions? What kind of world is it that throws parties for those that mess things up while leaving the faithful out plowing the fields?

The older brother then stands outside the door refusing to join the party. In doing so he too, like his younger brother, is separated, but this time not by greed, or shame, or guilt. The foreign land that he is lost in is the one of jealousy and judgment. And although he may be standing just outside the door of the party, he is as far away as his younger brother ever was. The story ends with the father showing the older brother that the same extravagant, reckless, prodigal love is for him too. But he must choose it for himself, and so it is for all of us.

This parable invites us to make the turn toward home. It invites us to make the choice to enter the party. It invites us to embrace the love that God has for all of us regardless of who we are, where we have been, or what we have done, whether we are the younger son or the older son. Because God's love for us is relentless and reckless and prodigal.

The young son was not propelled homeward because he felt worthy. It was because he felt broken. Maybe it is the same for you; I know it is for me. And when we come to God in brokenness and humility – like the son when he appeared on the horizon after his long journey home only to see his father running towards him with tears of joy streaming down his face – so too will we discover God waiting, ready to greet us with a Divine kiss. In that moment the party begins, and all the company of heaven rejoices. Because we were once lost and now, we are found. We were once far off in a foreign land and now we are home, at last.

Where do you see yourself in this story? Have you been the younger daughter/son?

Have you been the older son/daughter?

What does this parable say about the nature of God?

Blessed Am I Among Women

One Sunday during worship at the Century Regional Detention Facility (CRDF) – the adult women's jail in Lynwood – the Gospel lesson for the day was Jesus' teaching about marriage and how we will understand things differently in the age to come. The discussion that emerged was about how things would be different in heaven and what love would look like with no strings attached.

Constance talked about what she called *The Twin Flame*. She said that in her view, the world in which we live is greatly divided. She spoke of the dualistic way of thinking that separates us instead of bringing us together, but in the next life, there would be no such division. She explained that for her, the Twin Flame is about balancing both the feminine and the masculine energies burning equally as the flame of love.

It is so refreshing and inspiring to hear a young woman articulate what many of us have known through intuition and history has shown – that those things are out of balance – and it is largely due to the scales being weighted toward the masculine, patriarchal mindset that has repressed the feminine for too long. This has been true in the church, in the political arena, and societal structures through centuries and into our current time. It has not served – and is not serving – us well. Thankfully, many people are awakening to the importance of bringing the Divine Feminine into proper relationship in all of our understanding, whether in the church or in the world at large.

The rational, reasonable, analytical ways of the mind are valuable. After all, God gave us brains to use. But this *head space* is very different from the *heart space*, which is seen as more life-giving, nurturing, intuitive in nature. It's not that either is "good" or "bad," which is just another way of division through dualistic thinking. It's that we are out of balance. We should not supplant one for the other; we do not throw the baby out with the bath water! We would do well to bring things into a healthier, holistic spiritual balance that embraces both the Divine Feminine and the Sacred Masculine.

Many now realize what the mystics of all traditions have known and been trying to tell us for centuries. It is the deep wisdom of the Divine Feminine in relationship with that of the Sacred Masculine – which is the totality of the nature of God – that will lead us away from violence and into peace. This is intuitive, compassionate, and nurturing love energy that transcends the rational and reasonable mind and flows from the expansive heart of the Beloved.

To fully embrace both the Divine Feminine and the Sacred Masculine, it is essential that we embrace these two non-dual realities within ourselves. After all, are we not created in God's own image? The powerful feminine and the beautiful masculine live within each of us in harmony, but for far too long, especially in Western culture, we have been conditioned to try and divide and separate what is a unitive reality.

To fully embrace our whole nature as both feminine and masculine seems to be particularly challenging for men. Notice that above, I mention the *powerful feminine* and the *beautiful masculine*. Does this sound counter-cultural? I want to think not, but I suspect it does, because we have been conditioned to think in terms of women as beautiful and men as powerful, but in an unhelpful way of understanding. Our world has suffered too long the toxic effect of unbalanced masculine rule and male power, but things are changing.

In her amazing new book *Wild Mercy – Living the Fierce and Tender Wisdom of the Women Mystics*, Mirabai Starr states what has long needed to be realized. She says this:

> *Women do not always feel comfy inside traditional religious institutions. That's probably because the architecture of the world's organized religions and the furniture with which they are appointed have been designed largely by and for men. These structures are built to fit and uphold a male-dominated paradigm. Such boy-shaped arrangements no longer preclude a place for women who wish to sit there, however. Across the faith traditions women are being initiated, ordained, and sanctioned as rabbis and acharyas, priests and priestesses, ministers and murshidas, lamas and shamans. We are disrupting the balance of power and re-*

> *organizing the conversation. Increasing numbers of men, secure in their positions of privilege and authority, are voluntarily abdicating their power and handing it over to women, calling God "she" from the pulpit, seeding the academy with female philosophers. The alienation of women is as obvious to them – and as perilous – as it is to the women who have been historically excluded from positions of leadership.*

When Constance offered her interpretation of love without strings attached as the Twin Flame, she turned a lot of heads, not because what she said was hard to grasp, but instead the opposite. It was truth that cut to the heart of the matter in clear and concise terms that everyone could understand and embrace. It is no surprise that this wisdom came from a young woman who has known gender discrimination all of her life. She is in stride with the female mystics before her, and we were all touched by her prophetic wisdom.

Blessed am I among women.

Pilgrimage

Photo: Dennis Gibbs

Hundreds of millions of people set out on pilgrimages each year, visiting thousands of sacred sites around the world including holy places such as Jerusalem, Mecca, and the Ganges River in India. There are also the less traditional, yet no less spiritually-affecting sites that people are drawn to because it opens a connection with God as they understand God. Natural wonders such as The Grand Canyon, Native American lands, and memorials such as the Vietnam War Memorial in Washington D.C. or the National September 11 Memorial and Museum in New York City, are holy sites for millions.

The spiritual practice of pilgrimage is engrained in the human experience. Often when we think of pilgrimage, we think of a journey to sacred places, but pilgrimage is never just about the trek to a physical destination point. It is also, and maybe even more so, about the journey within us that will take us through the terrain of the human heart and plumb the depths of our being. Along the way, we may have a sense that we are closer to our most authentic self and closer to God.

The reasons that people embark on pilgrimages are as diverse as those who embark on them. Like the characters in *The Wizard of Oz* (a true pilgrimage story if there ever was one), some seek meaning in their lives, some seek their heart's desire, some search for their true selves. Others need healing. Some may feel the need to find their authentic home. Make no mistake, a pilgrimage is not vacation travel, nor is it a casual pedestrian stroll. Pilgrimages most always begin with a call or a deep yearning, an urgency to go, with intention to seek and find that which connects us most deeply with God and brings meaning and purpose to our life. The trip can be taken with our feet, but also within our hearts.

Once, on a trip to Mexico, I visited the Basilica of Our Lady of Guadalupe. The Feast of Our Lady of Guadalupe is on December 12th, but on the twelfth day of each month of the year, thousands of pilgrims make their way to Mexico City and the Basilica. It was a powerful experience to see thousands of people from different and distant places moving through the streets towards the Basilica. At one point, I turned to see two women entering the Basilica and moving toward the shrine, walking on their knees.

I watched for just a moment, but then had to turn away. The women's personal experience was theirs alone and I did not want to intrude upon it in any way.

I learned something about pilgrimage in that moment, that touched something deep within me. Maybe it was the ping of the homing device within that longs for my true home in the heart of God. I believe that that divine homing device is within all of us and guiding us, calling us home. Whether we are trekking across land, sitting in a sanctuary, or praying in a jail cell, the beckoning is the same because it is that of God which seeks a heart that will never rest until it finds its home.

Where is your pilgrimage? Where do you find your True Self?

A West Mountain Psalm

I come early to you Lord
with the rising of the sun
and the tall trees
my priests.
The fire is burning
and dancing
like my desire and praise.

The smoke is rising like incense.
The good morning song of the hawk
joining in prayer.
I listen in the stillness
of your cathedral
on the west mountain,
oh Great Spirit
I hear you,
for you are with me.

West Mountain

It's early fall on the West Mountain of the Cascades. I am alone at my brother Bob's cabin for a week or so, surrounded by the tall pine trees in this cathedral of God's creation in nature. Everything is turning red, yellow, gold, and brown. It's spectacular.

The neighboring cabins all seem unoccupied; I haven't seen another human being since my arrival three days ago. Fine with me. Not that I'm antisocial – not in an unhealthy way, anyway – but I came here with the intention to be alone.

The beauty, stillness, and hospitality of the wilderness here is quieting. The only sounds are of the occasional breeze moving through tress, and the far-off call of the hawk. The crested blue jays have already come to expect that I have with me an ample supply of wild bird seed and raw unsalted peanuts in the shell. Nothing beats food as an offering of hospitality, and the jays are not shy about accepting it. The chipmunks, on the other hand, are a bit more skittish and quite happy eating the numerous small pinecone pods that fall from the trees.

I arrived here with the energy of the world trailing me, and it has taken these three days to gently power down and quiet my internal self. I sense that the wild creatures, the trees, and all life here in this natural cathedral can feel the intrusion of civilization that follows a person here. I have been offering my prayer and asking forgiveness for any imposition, and I feel this place has heard me and is welcoming me as a friend. It makes me think about what my offering of peace and friendship might be.

I've been building a fire in the outdoor firepit each morning and praying Lauds, also known as Morning Prayer. Psalm 148 comes alive in a different way here: *sun and moon, shining stars, all mountains and hills, trees, beasts, small creatures and birds on the wing... let them praise the name of the Lord.*

Conversion of Life

The turning of one's heart and will to God does not happen suddenly. Instead, it is a way of life. It is not an enhancement of life, but a gradual movement toward becoming authentically human, created in God's image. It requires patience and persistence. There are no quick fixes or express lanes, just the constant and gentle turning to God, and it is a lifelong journey.

As we seek to evolve, transform, and grow in grace by turning away from self-will and turning toward the will of God, it is helpful to see ourselves as the pilgrim, guided by the Holy Spirit, living in ongoing conversion, mindful that God calls us into deeper places with ongoing newness and fullness of life. This means that we must also confront those parts of ourselves from which we need liberation: things like anger, judgment, the need for control, or unhealthy needs for affection or acceptance by others. We must be free from these things to realize the *Imago Dei* – the image of God – in which we were created. In doing so, we are free to change and become agents of transformation, not only in our own lives, but in the lives of others. The goal must always be to grow deeper in love of God and of our neighbor. It means that we are aware and open to the change required for the true conversion of life that can help us live closer to our true nature as created by God.

This conversion means that we will sometimes need to re-imagine ourselves in a way that helps us move our perceptions beyond what we know as our finite lives and into the wider view of the created universe. We may have to move past what we think we know into what we truly do not know – into the mystery – and trust that the Holy Spirit is leading us to deeper, richer places within the heart of God.

Our journey in life can offer us "conversion moments" within the larger trajectory of our lives. Remember Paul on the road to Damascus, and the blind man healed by Jesus' muddy touch. These experiences were powerful and profound, and yet like experiences in our own lives, they are moments that are not an end in themselves. They are moments that change the direction of our lives and set us on a new path – a longer road of self-discovery and transformation that leads us into a new understanding of who we are.

This path of life is not always an easy one to travel and it presents us with many challenges. The conversion road can lead through sorrow and through joy; through the desert and the oasis; through the dark night and into the sunlight of the Spirit. On this road we will drink from both the cup of tears and the cup of salvation, and all is a gift from God because it is the gift of life itself. Let us claim it all as our conversion experience as we press on, constantly changing and ever growing with a commitment to become the person God desires us to be.

Reflect on conversion moments that changed the direction of your life.

Stormy Seas
MARK 4:35-41

Photo: Dennis Gibbs

President John F. Kennedy kept a plaque on his desk in the Oval Office throughout his administration. Engraved into the plaque was the Breton Fisherman's Prayer, which reads:

> *Oh God, thy sea is so great*
> *and my boat is so small.*

There is a story in the New Testament that has the disciples in a frail little boat, tossed by the stormy waters of the enormous and powerful sea. They are understandably gripped by fear. The reaction of the disciples resonates with many of us. The swirling winds and churning waves that assail our fragile vessels – whether they be our personal, community, or national life – can inspire fear and uncertainty.

The correlation between this miracle story of Jesus calming the storm and our own lives seems obvious. The sea, the storm, and the fragile craft that carried Jesus and the disciples on their journey across the sea of Galilee offer metaphorical images of our journey in life – the perils at some turns, the vulnerability of the craft that carries us, and our own longing for the One who can calm not only the storms around us, but also those within us. On the surface, the parallels seem clear, but looking closer can take us into deeper waters of awareness.

One is that this story takes place on opposite shores of the Sea of Galilee. When Jesus said "Let's go across to the other side" he was suggesting more than just a trip to the other side of the lake. To travel to the other shore was to travel to the land of the Gentiles – the land of the Gerasenes, the land of non-Jews. He and his companions crossed the border into a foreign land beyond their own. This is a clear demonstration that his mission extends beyond the Jews. To set out for this opposite shore means that he is reaching out to strangers. This is a move of radical hospitality that says the Kingdom of God is for all people, not just those inside our own house.

Another thing to note is the language that Jesus uses when talking about fear. He never says that there is nothing to fear or to not be afraid, but instead asks, "Why are you afraid?" Life and its sometimes-stormy nature will always offer us plenty of opportunities to be frightened. The disciples had good reason to be afraid, and sometimes we do too. Jesus is asking us to name our fear; to not deny it or run away from it, but to be honest about what is happening within us when things get rough. Being people of God, or for that matter, being Christian, doesn't grant us immunity from being human.

Naming our fear is an invitation to get real with ourselves about the true nature of our being. Surely, we can reflect on where God is amid the storm, and what it means to still be alive on the other side of a situation that felt dangerous or even life-threatening. But we are also challenged to reflect on the deeper, insidious fear that resides well below the surface of the temporary passing storm. This allows us to reflect on what it truly means to be God's people, knowing that we have no special dispensation for an easy, storm-free life.

I think there is danger in the Pollyanna-type thinking that claims that if we just have enough faith, that if we *just* keep thinking positively, that if we are *just* good enough Christians, then God will protect us. Unfortunately, life does not work like that. It is a paradox of life that God does not always rescue us yet will hold us close in the midst of the storm, and even when things result in a tragic and heartbreaking end, God is with us through it all. This points us to why it is so important to get real with ourselves about our fears and our faith, and not settle for some Hallmark card version of spirituality. This work – and our spiritual life is indeed work – will help get us in touch with our true authentic selves and allow us to live on life's terms with grace and authenticity.

I have met many people in jails and prisons whose lives have been one very bad storm after another. In many cases, they were born into circumstances which never afforded them someone to turn to and trust – someone to help navigate the storm.

I never try to talk them out of their circumstances, never try to tell them it is all okay, because it is not. I simply get into the boat with them and remind them that they are not alone, and they are not forgotten. Many have never had someone who was willing to sit with them in the midst of the storm. They have never had someone that cared enough to listen to their questions about fear, and faith, and God – to listen to their longing and their heartache. And so, we sit together in our little boat, and we listen to each other, and we love. And sometimes, little by little, the storm begins to pass.

Faith is more than just believing that God will keep us safe. It is not the belief that God will rescue us, but the awareness that God hangs in there with us when the skies grow dark and the winds start howling. It is truly knowing that our struggle is God's struggle. Our fear is God's fear. Our broken heart is God's broken heart. It is knowing that God is always with us.

What storms have you faced in life? Who was willing to sit with you in times of trouble?

Have you sat with others in the storm of their lives?

What did you learn about yourself in these experiences?

Prayer
MARK 1:35

Photo: Chris Tumilty

I am clergy in the Episcopal Church. I am also a monk dedicated to my life of prayer. Others sometimes assume that people like me have deep insightful wisdom to offer about prayer. Do not be disappointed when I say that I do not. It is not for me to tell anyone how to connect with God. All I can genuinely offer is my own experience, which has taught me that there are as many ways to pray as there are human hearts beating for God.

I spent a good deal of time alone as a kid. Not that I was lonely; I have just always been comfortable in solitude.

Maybe I simply enjoy my own company, but I think there is more to it than that. There is something about the space of solitude that settles the soul and invites the Quieting of God. The important thing is to remain open and true to yourself. God will meet you there. Being alone in silence with God is my preferred way to pray.

This is not to say that I do not value prayer spoken with words. I do. In the monastery or in church gatherings, there are many prayers that we say together, and they help connect us in a communal way to God. In group worship, the intercessory prayers have a way of gathering the hearts of all present and bringing power to prayer in a way that is different than praying on one's own. Once while attending the Alcoholics Anonymous World Convention in Minneapolis, I held hands along with 50,000 people gathered in the Metrodome reciting the Lord's Prayer. It was exhilarating. I will never forget the stunning awareness of the Holy Spirit moving through that moment. Still, as amazing as that moment was, the Divine Spirit moves just as powerfully in the individual heart with the same quiet exhilaration.

In over two decades as a jail chaplain, I have prayed with thousands of my friends living behind the wall. I have felt the grace of God quiver our hearts and wet the faces of suffering with tears, cleansing our souls. We have held each other so close that it is hard to distinguish one trembling heartbeat from the other. Men have collapsed into my arms as I buoyed the weight of their sorrow and contrition. In these moments, life has never felt so real. We have never felt so seen by each other and felt so utterly loved by God. This is the power of prayer. It's not about just asking God to remove our suffering; it is about the opening of ourselves to allow for the grace and comfort of God who is in the thick of it with us – in full solidarity with us.

When people ask me for prayer, my first response is to ask them what is going on in their lives. The prayer begins with their answer to that question. My job is simply to see them, be with them, acknowledge their circumstances before God, and to pray for God's protection, grace, and peace to be with them. In the end, my hope is that I can be a brother to my friends, while staying out of the way enough to allow for God's grace to do its thing. That has worked pretty well for me for a long time, so I think I will stick with it.

In recovery, we say that we cannot transmit something that we do not possess. The same is true for prayer. If our prayer life is a little wobbly, that is what we have to offer. If, however, our prayer life is grounded in what is really real and connects us deeply with God, then we can offer that to the world.

I truly believe that ultimately, how I go about the living of my life is my prayer to God. That is better news on some days than others. Thomas Merton once said that our desire to please God indeed pleases God. That surely feels right.

Rain

The forecast of life calls for a 100 percent chance of occasional showers. Sometimes the rain is cold and unrelenting, chilling us to the bone. Other times it is a warm and gentle caress from above. At times, water falls from our eyes because our pain or joy is too much to bear. All are divine waters both tormenting and soothing, necessary for cleansing and healing.

Just as there can be no Easter resurrection without first the storm clouds of crucifixion and death, so it takes both rain and sun to create the glistening rainbow. When we have experienced the dark clouds of life, we can more greatly appreciate the freshness of the air after the last drop has fallen and the sun breaks upon us.

Welcome rain. Welcome sun. Welcome life.

Sabbath

*There is more to life than
merely increasing its speed.*

- Gandhi

It is an early June morning in 2019 and I am writing this from the Sabbath Road. About a month ago, I began a ten-week sabbatical. Now I sit in a cozy little Airbnb near Pismo Beach, California, with the cool ocean breeze and the welcoming sound of the waves.

For those unfamiliar, a sabbatical experience is an extended time away from normal obligations. It is a time to rest, refresh and renew our spirit. While a Sabbath day is just that – one day – a Sabbatical is a much larger period of time we give ourselves, usually anywhere from a few weeks to a few months. This extended time of Sabbath is essential to maintaining a healthy balance of life. The intention is to truly take time for ourselves and return to our vocations well-rested, more grounded, and with an ease of clarity about the life to which we return.

In my case, I use my time to write, read, pray, be in quiet solitude, and take in the local dining fare (nothing beats fresh fish and chips on the ocean front). I usually find the nearby A.A. Meetings and make myself a regular, even if for just a week or so. No matter where I am, those rooms always feel like home.

Since I am sort of a free agent for these few months, I am also traveling around California. Over the past few weeks, I have visited a monastery in Santa Barbara, made a trip into the desert at Joshua Tree, and am now resting at the ocean. Next, I will head south to Big Bear for some time with the big trees. Through it all, my appointment planner has rested in the same place: on the desk in my cell at the monastery, closed and undisturbed. It is utter freedom to awake every day with nowhere to go and nothing in particular to do other than to just "be."

We live in a culture of busyness. How many times have we heard someone respond to the question of how they are doing with the all-too-frequent refrain of: "Oh, I'm so busy!" Often that response comes with a bit of pride attached – like it's some sort of a badge of honor, as if being busy is an indication of one's importance. Being overextended and overworked can drain the vitality from life. We end up being only half-present, if present at all, for the truly important things and most of all for ourselves.

The Trappist Monk Thomas Merton said this:

"There is a pervasive form of contemporary violence... activism and overwork. The rush and pressure of modern life are a form, perhaps the most common form, of its innate violence. To allow oneself to be carried away by a multitude of conflicting concerns, to surrender to too many demands, to commit oneself to too many projects, to want to help everyone in everything, is to succumb to violence. It destroys our own inner capacity for peace. It destroys the fruitfulness of our own work, because it kills the root of inner wisdom that makes work fruitful."

Sabbath time can be a revolutionary and life-giving antidote to the culture of busyness, and help turn us away from the violence of overwork and our seemingly endless desire to do more, have more, and achieve more. Sabbath is much more than a mere vacation. It is a way to remove the illusion of "false gods" and remember who we are and what we know. It helps us reunite with deeper wisdom that is found only in silence and serenity. It connects us to that peace that surpasses all understanding.

There is a story in the New Testament about Jesus commissioning his disciples to heal and perform miracles. Upon their return, they were busy with excitement to tell Jesus about all they had done – all they had accomplished. But he would have none of it.

He didn't take the bait. He didn't pat them on the back and say "good job." He didn't give them a gold star or a badge of honor. What he did was to simply tell them to go to a deserted place and rest. That is timeless wisdom for all of us; to continually take time away to rest and renew.

When we do that, we have truly accomplished something.

In our monastery chapel, Jesus' words *"Abide in me as I abide in you"* are inscribed above the entrance. Those words are a reminder that the kingdom of heaven is within us, vital and sacred in every moment. It reminds us that God is always with us and that when we go within to rest, God meets us there.

The busyness of the modern world, with its endless frenetic fury of *Look at Me, Buy Me, Do Me, Watch Me,* is designed to seduce us away from the inner peace that is at our natural core. Sabbath can be our refuge. Whether it is a sabbath moment in the middle of a hectic day or in the middle of our work week, or a sabbatical removal from it all for a few weeks or even months, it can be our personal sanctuary that leads to real life and freedom. But we must choose it for ourselves. Here's hoping, to all who read this, that you will give yourself a break and venture into a wide-open space waiting for you this very moment.

The Power of Powerlessness

My great friend and sponsor tells a story of how one day, before he began recovery from his alcoholism, he was pulled over by the highway patrol on the I-5 freeway near Glendale. Apparently, for whatever reason, Don was deemed a threat to the police that afternoon, to the extent that they felt they need to handcuff him to the guardrail. Don tells of how, quite unexpectedly, his cousin Bruce drove by, saw that it was Don, and pulled over to offer whatever assistance he might, explaining to the police that Don and he were cousins. As he approached, Don yelled out, "It's OK, Bruce! I have everything under control!"

I think all of us can see the humorous yet sad truth in this story: how many of us, still in the grip of our disease, fooled ourselves into thinking that everything was under control, when in truth, everything was coming apart at the seams. As addicts, we know the calamity of this self-deception, not from an abstract point of view but from actual experience. Many of us have had situations as absurd as Don's, where we clung to the illusion of power and control but in reality were handcuffed by the disease of our addiction.

The Big Book of Alcoholics Anonymous talks about the lack of power being our dilemma. I think when new friends in recovery hear this; they might feel confused and say, "Wait a minute – first you say that the lack of power is my dilemma and then you say that I am to admit that I am powerless?" On the surface, this may seem to be a contradiction, but it is not. There is difference between being *powerful* and being *empowered*. There is a difference between the illusion of earthly power that is the quest of the human ego, and the spiritual power that is the quest of God.

I venture to say that it was the ego's quest for power that spoke from the guardrail that day. And if Don's experience is anything like mine, there may have been a different voice whispering that day, a voice that only he could hear: a voice that was tired of the illusion, a voice that was longing for relief, a voice of powerlessness.

It is in moments like these that we are confronted with the dilemma of the illusion of power and the quest of the unrestrained ego versus the desire of God's will, sometimes realized through the surprising gift of powerlessness. In these moments, we are offered a choice to continue the quest of the ego for the illusion of power and control or to release ourselves from the quest and give ourselves to the desire of God's will for us. It is the surrendering of the false self to the True Self that God created us to be. This giving of ourselves to God's will is what Jesus is referring to when he speaks of the *narrow gate.*

"Enter by the narrow gate; for the gate is wide and the way is easy that leads to destruction, and those who enter it are many. For the gate is narrow and the way is hard that

leads to life, and those who find it are few."

For alcoholics, the reckless way of self-destruction, littered with heartache and despair, is the path on which we found ourselves. For me, it started innocently enough; it was fun to be cool and drink and get high. I felt so much in control. Then it snuck up on me. I was trapped like Don had been that day, handcuffed by my addiction yet still claiming everything was under control. Then, just when I was on the verge of giving into death, by the grace of God I found the narrow gate that led to recovery, and to new life.

The gate is indeed narrow, and only for a few does it lead to life. *Finding* the gate is only the beginning; *entering* the gate is another matter, just as getting sober is only the beginning, and engaging in the deeper work of spiritual growth in recovery is a different matter. Sobriety is *finding the gate*. Recovery is *entering the gate*, and sadly, few make it. The Big Book says it clearly: many who relapse do so because they failed to enlarge their spiritual life. They settled for simply finding the gate of sobriety and could not, for whatever reason, enter through the narrow path of spiritual growth that is essential to recovery.

The sad truth is that roughly one in ten people are afflicted with the disease of alcoholism and/or drug addiction, and only a very few ever find the gate that could lead them to a better life. And of those who do find it, only about 10% or less are able to achieve long-term recovery from this *"seemingly hopeless state of mind and body."* Those that do have done so because they have entered the narrow gate. They have not settled for mere sobriety. They have let go of the ego's quest for the illusion of power and have not only admitted, but know in their innermost selves, that they are powerless and have become empowered by that truth. This stunning revelation opens the gate wide for a complete spiritual transformation. This power is not born of illusion that is the quest of the ego, but the transformative power of God accessed through the narrow gate of recovery.

This is the real power of powerlessness.

Blessed are those who find it.

Canticles of Hope

Canticles are scripture set to song. Two of the most familiar are the Magnificat, also known as the *Song of Mary*, and the Benedictus, or the *Song of Zechariah*. Each one in its own way inspires hope, not only in the times in which they were written, but also for our own time as well. In a very real sense, they, like all of scripture, are timeless.

THE MAGNIFICAT
The Song of Mary
LUKE 1: 46-55

Young Mary set out to visit her cousin Elizabeth, knowing that she, like herself, was pregnant. Upon her arrival, as she drew nearer to Elizabeth, the unborn children began leaping in what was nothing other than divine joy. What a moment that must have been. On that day, not only did the two in the womb leap with joy, but so did the mothers. I can only imagine the look on their faces, the bursting with joy. Mary was so ecstatic that she began to shout out her song that would become known as the Magnificat. She sang praise to God who had blessed her. She sang out gratitude for grace. She sang out in humility.

Mary became a prophet of hope in that moment, announcing how the child within would topple tyrants and bring the powerful to their knees, while giving to the poorest and leaving the rich standing empty. She was talking about the coming reign of the justice of God through her child. Could it be that she was also speaking to her unborn child, like mothers through the ages have spoken to their children in the womb? If you believe that an inborn infant can hear the voice of their mother or father from within the womb, then you might believe that Jesus heard his mother's prophetic call to him.

We will know true justice has been accomplished not when the privileged among us know it, but when the most marginalized and vulnerable know it. When those who struggle – the prisoners, the immigrants, our LGBTQ brothers and sisters – gain justice, then it will be real. Mary was saying that the infant that would burst from her womb is the human and divine instrument of God's mercy and justice, and that is real good news for every marginalized person in the world both then and now.

Mary may have entered the biblical scene as an unknown, unwed young woman, but she becomes a powerful, prophetic voice of the coming of God's reign. Hers is a clarion song for disenfranchised people – those relegated to the margins – that says that the oppressors will not stand in the Kingdom of God and that God will raise up those cast down. Mary's Magnificat pulls the disempowered to their feet, lifting their faces to the sunlight of the Spirit of God. Mary's song is one of hope.

THE BENEDICTUS
The Song of Zechariah
LUKE 1:68-79

Imagine the scene: the Baptist infant has been born to Mary's cousin Elizabeth. As was the Jewish custom, all were gathered on the eighth day after his birth for the circumcision and naming of the child. Everyone assumed that the infant would be named Zechariah in honor of his father, as was also the custom. But Elizabeth stunned those gathered by proclaiming that her newborn son would be named John. Those present then turned to Zechariah hoping for him to settle the issue. Zechariah had been rendered mute by the Archangel Gabriel because he had doubted the angel's proclamation nine months earlier. When asked about the naming, he requested a writing tablet, on which he wrote, "His name shall be John."

The people were astounded. And so it was that the infant cousin of Jesus, who would become the prophetic Baptist, was named John. That is when Zechariah's voice came back to him, and he immediately began to praise God with the words that we know as the *Song of Zechariah*, or the *Benedictus*.

Zechariah first praises God for bringing a Savior, giving thanks for the prophets and sages who proclaim truth, and keeping the promise made to our ancestors to protect the people, and bringing freedom for those persecuted for their faith.

Then, Zechariah turns to his newborn son, and speaks of what he will become – a prophet and clarion voice for the coming reign of God's justice; that God's light will shine from him onto those buried in darkness as he walks the way of peace. These are powerful visionary words, and they are as much about us as they were about John. This song speaks to the hope that has come to us through God. It is a hope that has been offered through the ages of promises and prophets that still lives with us today.

Each morning, when we pray Lauds at the monastery, we recite the Benedictus. It is a powerful way to start each day, because we are not only reminded of what God has done through John and Jesus, but also of our own call. Are not we all called to be a John the Baptist in our own life? Isn't it true that to be a follower of Jesus in the most authentic way means that we will also prepare the way for the path to salvation and truth? We too are called to show others the way of compassion, forgiveness, and hope. Through living in this way, we will surely know peace and be able to offer it to the world. The Benedictus is first about the hope for justice and peace that God has brought into the world. Secondly, it is about the hope that each of us can share with one another.

Both the Magnificat and the Benedictus mark an important shift in the Biblical narrative away from judgment and wrath toward compassion, mercy, justice, and love. Surely, we have a long way to go to bring about world peace, but as followers of the way of Jesus, we can be the voice crying out in the wilderness. We can be the instruments of God's grace. We can prepare the way for the Prince of Peace to enter people's hearts. Together, we can help make the world a better place.

This is the authentic Gospel life.

Prophetic Truth & Power

MATTHEW 14:1-12

The story of the beheading of John the Baptist is filled with desire, betrayal, corruption, vengeance and eventually, John's head on a platter. It has all the elements of a great Shakespearean tragedy. But this story is not the poetic product of a playwright's imagination. This is a glimpse into the nature of the human condition and what can – and does – sometimes happen when prophetic truth speaks to misguided structures of power. And surely John is among the most important prophets of old, acknowledged when Jesus said that no one born of a woman is greater than John the Baptist.

Many people throughout the ages have been identified as prophetic voices of their time, though most fall short of the true definition of the classic biblical prophets. From religious leaders to political figures, poets to street-corner evangelists, many have been called prophets or thought so of themselves. In today's modern-day perception, the term prophet may be overused and too casually assigned, and as a result we may have lost, at least to a degree, the meaning and power of true prophesy and the nature of those who bring such a voice of truth. On the other hand, we should also understand that each of us, in our own way, are called to bring a prophetic voice to our world.

Interestingly, some cultural figures of the modern age have proven to carry important messages of justice, peace, compassion and love. Certainly, individuals such as Dr. Martin Luther King, Jr., Gandhi, Dorothy Day, Mother Teresa and Thomas Merton were important historical figures and powerful prophetic voices in our time. The wisdom of our Native American forefathers and mothers whisper to us in the wind. Today, the Reverend William Barber is a voice of justice for the poor and Greta Thunberg is speaking environmental truth to world powers that threaten our planet. Young people like Emma Gonzalez lead the call for an end to gun violence. I also hear brave and bold voices coming from behind the walls of incarceration, shedding light on the darkness of the industrial prison complex.

Prophets always live within the tension between loyalty to truth and compassion for the community in which they preach. They often pay a great price for their commitment to justice, peace and dignity for all, and sometimes the price is their very life. John was beheaded, Jesus was crucified, Gandhi and King were assassinated. All stood for the poor, the marginalized and the disenfranchised. All stood against the abuse of power, racism, bigotry, poverty and oppressive structures that diminished human dignity. All stood for truth, and all were in a way like John – the voice crying out in the wilderness. Lastly, it could be said that all were following a prophetic call from God. These prophets of our age were, like those of scripture, not without flaws. They were not gods; they were human. One does not need to be perfect to be an instrument of truth. All of us can use our voice.

For us to follow Jesus, the call of our baptism as Christians means that when Jesus looks government or religion or society squarely in the eye and says "Something is wrong," we too can never accept the status quo if others are injured or treated unjustly, or marginalized because of national, societal or religious interests. Like John the Baptist, when we see something happening in front of us that works against human dignity, we must speak truth to power even if it means our heads might be handed over on a platter.

As monks in the Community of Divine Love monastery, our primary ministry is as spiritual companions with our friends locked up in jails and prisons. It is our way of responding to the prophetic call of Jesus to visit him in prison. It echoes Isaiah 61, which says that *"the spirit of the Lord GOD is upon us, because the Lord has anointed us; he has sent us to bring good news to the oppressed, to bind up the broken-hearted, to proclaim liberty to the captives and release to the prisoners; to proclaim the year of the LORD's favor, and the day of vengeance of our God; to comfort all who mourn; to provide for those who mourn in Zion— to give them a garland instead of ashes, the oil of gladness instead of mourning, the mantle of praise instead of a faint spirit."*

But this prophetic call is not just for monks. It is a call for all of us to commit to the work of justice and peace. If you are wondering if and when you will be anointed, you already have been. It happened at your birth.

If the baptismal vow to strive for justice, peace and dignity for all is our prophetic vision statement, then our mission statement can be found in Matthew 25. We are to feed the hungry, quench the thirty, welcome the stranger, clothe the naked, take care of the sick and visit the prisoner, because when we do these things, we do them for him. He is the stranger in our midst. He is the one locked up in jail. He is the homeless person and the lost teen on the street. Jesus then goes on to do what all prophets do: He warns about the grave consequences of not heeding his call.

If all of this seems a bit much, remember this: we were never promised it would be easy, just that it would be worth it. This is what it means to answer the call and to become ourselves prophets of peace in our own time and in our own place. We too are called to bring a human voice to God's truth, to speak God's words through the prophets of old, through the prophets of our own time — the street corner prophet, the coffee house prophet, the prophet in the pew, the prophet behind bars, and the prophet in you.

Can you see yourself as a prophet in your own time and circumstance?

Prophets of Peace

I began to write this on the national observance that honors the life of the Reverend Martin Luther King, Jr. As it is for so many, his role in the American Civil Rights movement, and his call to nonviolent resistance as the means to achieve social justice, is a constant source of inspiration.

The America of King's time was different from that of the twenty-first century in which we live, yet we are still plagued with the same issues of racism and inequality. In the 50s and 60s, the Jim Crow laws that sanctioned the oppression of people of color forced our African American sisters and brothers to live less than the life for which they were created. During the later years of his life, King's prophetic witness extended beyond the racism that plagued the soul of humankind and into the issues of poverty and war – particularly the Vietnam War – that also tore away at the moral fabric of our society.

Martin Luther King inspired real change in our country

and in the world. As a result of his commitment to true justice and civil rights, the rising voice of the people inspired legislative change to ensure a degree of equality among all people of this nation. Perhaps more importantly, he changed how our African-American brothers and sisters, as well as all oppressed peoples looking on, saw themselves. He helped to restore and protect human dignity. He reminded all oppressed people that they were *somebody*. He reminded us that we – *everybody* – are all created in the image of God.

Like with all true spiritual leaders, King's civil rights vison was born of a faith rooted deep within him. It was the unwavering moral conviction of his beliefs as a Christian that inspired his leadership. It was the contemplation of the core values of his faith that propelled him into action. This is essential truth because protests without this contemplative core are just noise, but true, real change comes only from first giving oneself to deep listening to God's desire for us. This is why the Reverend Martin Luther King was so grounded in his truth, a truth that had the power to eventually change the moral compass of our country.

As an Episcopal Christian, I look to the life and teachings of Jesus as core values. In our baptismal covenant, we vow to *"seek and serve Christ in all persons, to strive for justice and peace among all people, and to respect the dignity of every human being."* All persons, all people, every human being, with no exceptions. This is the type of moral compass that was at the heart of the Civil Rights Movement, those who accepted the leadership roles of that movement, and the people who were a part of it.

The Reverend Dr. Martin Luther King was not the first to conceive of a non-violent approach to oppression, nor was he the first to teach the power of loving your neighbor, especially your enemies. These teachings came from

Jesus; King took them to heart and reminded us all of who we are to be as Christians.

The divisions of our time are not unlike other times in history; however, our struggles with racial unrest and police brutality are more exposed than in the past due to video technology and fast-moving information. Some rightly feel that the very moral fabric of our nation is at stake. Just as we needed prophetic voices to spark the Civil Rights movement sixty years ago, we need them in our own time to point us back to the truth of who we are as individuals and as a nation. As Christians, we should take seriously what we were taught by the one whom we profess to follow. The core values are simple and yet can have a profound effect on the direction of our common life: justice, peace, respect, dignity, radical forgiveness, and unconditional love – and yes, even love for those we are tempted to consider our enemies. If we can reconnect our moral and spiritual compass that points us to these values, we just might be able to stop yelling at each other and begin to listen. Once we do that, we are ready to love again.

Black Man in a Black Hole

JERAMIE, HAITI 2016

He is a black man in a black hole. He emerges from the shadows. All I can see is his searching eyes on me as I stand in the light of the shining sun, looking through the crude barred window of this Haitian prison cell, but I can immediately feel his beauty. It's troubling to see it encased in utter darkness. His gaze penetrates me with gentleness and kindness. It shortens my breath.

I've been around a lot of people locked in cages, but this is different, and all of the sudden I am not so steady, not so sure of why I'm here. I've never seen anything like this. After a moment I hand him a tiny piece of paper. On one side I had written *Senye we ou,* which is Creole for *God sees you.* He smiles like he knows it to be true. But do I? If God sees him, then why this? Why is he stuck in a black hole, living in filth with people packed in so tight there's no room to breathe?

The other side of the paper reads *Mwen we ou,* which means *I see you.* But is it true? Do I really see him? Is it even possible for me to really see him? I am standing out-side with an endless space in which to roam. He's with more than a dozen other men stuffed into a 30'x30' con-crete box in suffocating heat, with no clean water, no toi-let, no bed, no hope. Yet, the beauty in his eyes teaches me something. His smile almost makes mine feel inauthen-tic. Is this a mirror?

Can I really see him or am I just kidding myself? *Can you really see him? If you do, why don't you put a stop to this? Because what I see is an insult to your creation, a desecra-tion of human dignity. What I see feels like an abomina-tion. What I see makes me sick, and sad, and angry. Do you feel that way too? Where is your mercy in this place?*

He points to the paper. He looks up and does some-thing I cannot do in that moment: he smiles. I want to cry. Then he points first to his eyes and then to mine. He's telling me that he sees me too. He reaches through the bars and places his hand on my heart. The warmth of his touch moves through me and radiates from my eyes to his fixed gaze of gentleness and love. Then he takes my hand and pulls it into the shadows and places it on his heart. We are connected in a beautiful, mysterious friendship. I don't want to remove my hand. I don't want this moment to end. What do I really see in this black hole house of mirrors? Is it you? Is it me?

I am sure of one thing. Like the earth's shifting on the ocean floor, this encounter has changed something deep within me. I may not be fully aware of what that is, but I know that this is something deeper than compassion, a love that goes beyond my understanding, and yet is not beyond my *knowing*. I find a way to say farewell that day and step away, but there is no turning back from this mo-ment.

White Skin, Black Tears

I will never know how it feels for
my dark-skinned friends,
but I know that my tears are black.

Original art by Dennis Gibbs

"don't shoot" – "I can't breathe"
cry hearts of lives that matter
shame of white silence

This haiku speaks of the racial unrest that erupted in America after the murder of George Floyd at the hands of law enforcement, one in a long list of Black people killed by police in preceding years that caught national attention, including Rayshard Brooks, Daniel Prude, Breonna Taylor, Atatiana Jefferson, Aura Rosser, Stephon Clark, Botham Jean, Philando Castile, Alton Sterling, Michelle Cusseaux, Freddie Gray, Janisha Fonville, Eric Garner, Akai Gurley, Gabriella Nevarez, Tamir Rice, Michael Brown, Tanisha Anderson, and Ahmaud Arbery. Sadly, by the time you hold this book, more names will have been added to this list.

Floyd's murder on May 25, 2020 ignited outrage and cries for justice across the nation. The haiku above also points to the shameful complicity of white people's silence amid the bloodshed and killing of Black people in our country. This white silence must be broken. The first step is for people of white privilege to acknowledge that in enjoying the benefits of a system that favors white people and disfavors people of color, we contribute to systemic racism that disenfranchises people of color, leading to diminishment of life, brutality, and death, and continues to rip apart the fabric of our common life.

White, White Everywhere

White, white everywhere –
to the left and to the right
everywhere white
with bloody fingerprints
on their hymnals.

Remember Who You Are

There is a scene in *The Lion King* when the mystic healer Rafiki takes Simba to meet the spirit of his deceased father Mufasa, who before his death had been the beloved King of the Pridelands. Simba, growing up in exile, has lost touch with who he truly is. The spirit of Mufasa says to his son, "You have forgotten who you are and have so forgotten me. Look inside yourself, Simba. You are more than what you have become. You must take your place in the circle of life. Remember who you are. You are my son, and the one true King."

Remember who you are. Mufasa was telling his son to remember the kingship invested in him. The king's brother Scar, who had taken the throne through murder and deceit, has ruled in darkness with intimidation and violence. Mufasa tells his son that despite the authority that Scar holds, Simba has the inherent responsibility to challenge him. With those words, Mufasa releases the strength from within Simba to do the right thing.

This is a compelling fable that speaks to empowerment and dominion. Dominion should never be confused with domination. Domination – like that of Scar – uses tyranny to oppress and diminish the human spirit through fear and intimidation. *Dominion*, like that of Mufasa and Simba, uses leadership to build people up and empower them to be their most authentic selves that align with goodness and compassion. At the same time, dominion uses power to break the yoke of oppression that weighs down the most vulnerable and most marginalized among us.

At times of uncertainty and upheaval, we may be prone to acting in fear and confusion. This is when we need to find a way to take a step back and trust the voice of wisdom within each of us that can help us find our center again, the voice that reminds us who we are.

Who am I? This question is the starting block from which we can push off and begin to reclaim our true identity. For some people, the answer is that we are fundamentally created in the image of God – one of a life-giving spirit in love and compassion. When we can see ourselves in this way, then we begin to see others the same. All major faith traditions hold this truth.

As Christian people of God's family, we can look at the teachings of Jesus to help us understand our identity as, like Simba, heirs to the kingdom. One of those teachings is the Beatitudes, which describe those who inherit the kingdom of God as people who are poor in spirit, meek, merciful, pure in heart, and peacemakers. Then later, in Matthew's account of the Gospel, Jesus says that we are to feed the hungry, give water to the thirsty, welcome the stranger, clothe the naked, care for the sick, and visit the prisoner. It is in the living of this life that we can truly become awakened to who we have always been.

Each of us has tremendous ability and divine agency

within us to choose what is right – what is good. But the darkness around us can sometimes seem a lot like Scar: relentless in its death-dealing schemes and its claim to false dominion. Under that kind of tyranny, sometimes we, like Simba, forget that we have the right to challenge and bring about change. Jesus reminded us of this capacity when he once said that not only would we do things that he did, but even greater things. Do we believe that?

Claiming or reclaiming the inherent divine power within us is essential if we are to truly be agents of change in this moment in history. We must spend more time with ourselves – our True Selves that were created by God for goodness, for justice, and for compassion. We would do well to spend time disconnecting from that which is filled with deception, and more time connecting to the deep inner Mufasa that speaks the truth of God about not only who we are, but who we need to be. If we can reconnect with the still, small voice within that desires only peace, justice, and truth, we can change the world. When we make peace within ourselves, the world will make peace with us.

In the end, Simba finally returns to Pride Rock and assumes his rightful reign as King, but not because he plays Scar's game of lies and manipulation. He does not demand the love of the people through fear and intimidation as Scar has tried to do. Instead, the kingdom's subjects accept Simba as ruler for his compassion, his vision of truth, and his courage. All these things are realized within him because he is guided by the direction of his spirit father's mandate to remember who he is. Each of us has a Simba within us. Each of us can remember who we truly are and be guided by that truth.

Who/what has been the voice of Scar in your life? Who/ what has been the voice of Mufasa in your life?

Sewing a button
like she taught me on that day
I remember her

The nature of haiku is to reflect deeply on the moment and to allow wisdom to unfold and reveal itself. These transcendent moments can be deeply contemplative, almost as though time itself takes on new meaning.

This haiku emerges from a moment of memory. As I sat sewing a button on a worn, favorite shirt, the contemplative attention to the rhythm of needle and thread moving through the dark grey fabric and pushing through the tiny holes in the buttons transfixed me. In that silent rhythm, everything was still except the needle.

In this moment, I remembered the day long ago when my mother first taught me how to sew a button. I remembered the scent of her hair, her smile, and her careful and steady gaze on her own needle. I remember her fingers. It was a tender and loving visitation. It felt as though the mystery of time itself somehow knew that this moment would come back to me some fifty-five years later.

The bending and blending of time offer us these glimpses into a realm that we may never fully understand on an intellectual level, but they are deeply known in the intuitive self, if we will only pay close attention to seemingly simple things like a needle pulling thread through a button.

What moments in your life are pleasant memories for you?

October

For a large portion of my life, the months of the year went by without memorable markings on the calendar. However, since I began my recovery in 1998, almost every month holds memories to be revisited; some pleasant, some sad, some worthy of celebration.

The seasons of spring, summer, fall, and winter bring their own distinct character to the cycle of life. I love the freshness of spring, and the mountains and oceans under the summer sun. The shortening days and cooler nights of fall bring a distinct smell in the air that I love. The cold, dark nights of early winter remind me that Christmas is coming.

I also appreciate the cycles of the seasons of the church year and how they mark time in the spiritual life, returning year after year. The annual cycle of Advent, Christmas, Epiphany, Lent, Easter, and Pentecost have, in their annual returning, enriched my faith and deepened my sense of the mystery of God.

These intertwining cycles of the natural and the spiritual worlds are woven together by prayer, meditation, and contemplative practice in ways that allow me to know myself, heal from wounds, know love, and draw closer to God, yet another cycle returns annually to invite me into continued healing, self-awareness, and gratitude for the life of freedom that I live today.

It is October now. The time has come again.

The third of October marks for me the beginning of an annual cycle of remembrance. It was on that day in 1997 that my friend Kenny was murdered in a drug deal, shot through the head from the back seat of his own car. He was left slumped over the steering wheel at a stop light at the intersection of Laurel Canyon and Sherman Way in North Hollywood. That day was the beginning of a chain of events that would bring an end to my long downward spiral into the dark abyss of addiction.

It is common for people in recovery to remember those last dark days before we were able to get sober and make a beginning in recovery. For me, it begins in October and runs into January. Each year, the layers of self-awareness continue to unfold, and the path of healing becomes more and more complete.

I remember looking down at my buzzing pager. I remember calling Chris and being told Kenny was dead. I remember the mix of anger and sadness that grew deeper each day. I remember the days going to that intersection in my drug-induced frenzy and talking to everyone I could, trying to find out what happened, who saw anything, and who was responsible. I remember the looks of pity. During my life on the streets, I have had people cast many different looks my way – suspicious looks, angry looks, empty looks – but nothing affected me like those looks of pity coming from the eyes of people powerless over my inconsolable grief.

I remember the flower and candle memorial near the light pole. I remember placing my own offering and feeling like none of the others felt the stab of Kenny's death like I did. For many years during this time of remembering the events of October 1997, I would go to that intersection. I didn't really know why; something in me needed to go. After a few years of recovery, I came to realize that the place held nothing for me any longer, and left knowing it was finished.

The same has been true for other markers of those last few months of my active addiction. The bars we slung dope in. The last apartment I was evicted from. The places I slept in my car, or on cardboard. The supermarkets I stole booze and food from. The rear parking lot of the seedy bar where my car was taken from me at knifepoint, and the North Hollywood Hospital where my friend Tracy died of overdose. Over time, I have stopped visiting those places on my annual memorial tour, but I still remember. It is good that I never forget.

This year, I made one physical visit. It was to the building where the Radford Group used to meet, and where I walked into the A.A. Meeting on New Year's Eve in 1997. I sat down in the meeting that day, raised my hand as a newcomer, and said the words that I have repeated thousands of times since: "My name is Dennis, and I'm an alcoholic." That was the end of the nightmare. The next day I met Don, the man who became my lighthouse on the shore of my dark sea of despair, and the man who is still my sponsor today. That was the beginning of the dream that has become my life.

Yes, it is October. Soon the days will be cooler. Halloween will bring troops of children to the door for treats and maybe a trick or two up my sleeve. November is, for me,

Gratitude Month, when I am more intentional about re-flecting and expressing my thankfulness for the people and things that have come into my life. December will once again bring Christmas, my favorite time, with a set of its own more recent memories that one day will be re-visited.

January is the season of Epiphany in the church, which means "manifestation." It inspires me to think about how my life unfolds and manifests itself into the world around me. My sobriety date is also in January. It is a time for me to reflect on where I have been, what I have learned, and where I am going. It is good to let things go, to move on, and yet never forget.

Those last few months of 1997, the darkest of the dark night of my soul, now have become the high holy days that lead into the annual celebration of my sobriety and life in recovery – a true resurrection story of redemption and freedom that once seemed impossible. The cycle of life continues in recovery, in the church, and in the world one day at a time, with each creating new memories that will one day be revisited, each embracing the gift of life.

Soon enough it will be winter again, followed once again by the blossoming of spring. As the cycle continues to turn, it feels good to know that my life is complete.

the cycle of life
continues its unfolding
within and around

Joy Noel

In an unlikely place, under no ordinary circumstances, something extraordinary takes place. The scene is a stable in the dark of night. The characters are a poor, unwed Jewish teenager and the man to whom she is betrothed but not yet married. Shepherds and angels are in the fields. Mystics come from the east following a star. On this first day of Christmas, the Divine Child has come into the world. The blue dawn has broken. The light of peace has pierced the darkness.

Extraordinary moments can happen on Christmas Day. One of those moments occurred on December 25, 1914, in the trenches of the Western Front during World War I. On that clear, crisp Christmas morning, thousands of British, Belgian, and French soldiers stepped out of their trenches and spent the day mingling with their German enemies. Many have said that this moment in history was more than a mere happenstance, but a rare moment of peace, an extraordinary point of grace, in a war that would eventually take over fifteen million lives.

It started the night before on Christmas Eve. As Pvt. Albert Moren of the Queen's Regiment recalled in a found document, the night was *"a beautiful moonlit night, frost on the ground, white almost everywhere."* It is reported that it all began when the Germans started singing "Silent Night" with the Allies joining in.

Graham Williams of the Fifth London Rifle Brigade remembers it this way:

> *"First the Germans would sing one of their carols, and then we would sing one of ours, until when we started up 'O Come, All Ye Faithful' the Germans immediately joined in singing the same hymn to the Latin words Adeste Fideles. And I thought, well, this is really an extraordinary thing – two nations both singing the same carol in the middle of a war."*

The next morning, German soldiers emerged from their trenches calling out "Merry Christmas" in English. Allied soldiers came out to greet them. Others held up signs reading: "You no shoot, we no shoot." Over the course of the day, troops exchanged gifts of cigarettes, food, buttons, and hats. The Germans shared their beer with the Allied troops. The Christmas truce also allowed both sides to help each other bury their dead comrades, whose bodies were in the "no man's land" between opposing trenches.

While there were occasional moments of peace throughout the rest of World War I, they never again came of the scale of the Christmas Day truce of 1914.

This is a real-life story of the light of God's grace and peace penetrating man-made darkness, and it is a story that also speaks to us today more than a hundred years later as we struggle with our own forms of darkness and the atrocities brought on by war, terrorism and violence. As beautiful and powerful as the nativity story is for us in our lives, there also remains the harsh reality of the conditions in which we live and into which the Divine Word comes to us today. As wonderfully astonishing as it is that the Light shines in the darkness, there is still the reality of that darkness.

All major religions have at their foundation a theology of love and a commitment to peace. All have prophets, sages and gurus who guide their people into the ways of divine love – spiritual leaders such as Abraham, Gandhi, Muhammad, and The Dalai Lama. For Christians, the Avatar of Divine Light is Jesus.

Now, more than ever, we need to all work together. Now, more than ever, we need to set aside our differences and embrace each other as equally important to God's work. As Christians, this is our time – our moment – to offer to the entire world the Light of Lights, The Lord of Lords, the Prince of Peace, who now comes to all incarnate in human flesh and dwells with us in order to teach us – as John the Baptist foretold – to make smooth the ways of peace. Christmas is our opportunity to share with the world what that really means. This is our time to share with the world our Lord's teachings and to show that, as followers of Jesus, we are unwavering – as he was and is – to our commitment to justice, truth, dignity, peace, and love. That commitment extends to all people, regardless of religious affiliation. This is what it means to be a Christian.

We have known the tyranny of a death-dealing global pandemic that has forced separation from one another. We have come to a time of reckoning for racial injustice. Climate change is real and has brought our planet to a precarious edge. Violence all too often seems to rule the modern day. We desperately need to clear the way for peace. Christians, and our brothers and sisters from other religious traditions, can help lead the way.

The spirit of Christmas should not be boxed in to one day – or for that matter, into just the Christian box – because Christmas, in essence, is for the whole world. The spirit of peaceful accord should extend into all our days to all people and should continue beyond a single time of year. We have an opportunity every day to bring the good news to the world in ways that are vital, relevant, and that can help heal us as a global community of God's family.

Many of our friends in jails and prisons have become *Divine Companions* of our Community of Divine Love. They have committed themselves to a spiritual Rule of Life, a design for living that includes prayer, meditation, study of Scripture, and service to others. An important element of the Divine Companion Commitment is to non-violence, and to be peacemakers in the midst of a sometimes-chaotic environment. Our Divine Companion brothers and sisters do their part to be instruments of peace, and we are deeply grateful for their witness and striving to make the world of incarceration a better place.

In the Episcopal Church we will *"seek and serve Christ in all persons, loving our neighbors as ourselves... strive for justice and peace among all people, and respect the dignity of every human being."* To encounter all persons, all people, and every human being, we need to think and love beyond borders and divisions. This is a movement, a movement of God's revelation of love into all the world, to all the people of the world. This is about truly loving as Christ loved, inspiring the very best in people regardless of their denominational stripes or spiritual tradition. It's about respecting others in such a way that our Jewish, Muslim, Hindu, Buddhist, Sikh and other sisters and brothers in the world are able to claim, with authenticity and freedom, their own life and spiritual path to God because of our Christian presence, not in spite of it. It is about understanding that when we step out of our own trenches, the space between us need not be a no man's land, but instead an invitation to come together on common ground as one people. And like that Christmas Day in 1914, we just might find ourselves singing 'O Come, All Ye Faithful' together in peace.

This is how we show the world who we are as Christians. It is a statement that says we are all in this together and that regardless of our individual spiritual paths, we are all bound for the arms of God. There is a wonderful greeting offered to us from the Sanskrit language, contained in one word: *"Namaste,"* which means that *the Divine in me acknowledges and bows to the Divine in you.* It is in this beautiful unitive spirit that Christ lives. It is within this spirit that God calls us together as one. This is the Christmas spirit. And it is in this spirit that we can all clear the way for peace.

Doubt

JOHN 20:19-25

I heard a story once about a famous tightrope walker who amazed the crowds with his ability to walk across large expanses – waterfalls, canyons or between tall buildings – while never losing his balance, all to the delight and amazement of the crowd. When he returned to his starting point, he would ask the crowd if they believed he could go across and back again with a wheelbarrow. There were a few skeptics, but most believed that he could do it. He would then prove his amazing ability by taking the wheelbarrow with him on another round trip. When he returned, he would ask the crowd if they believed that he could do it with someone sitting *in* the wheelbarrow. By this time, the crowd was exuberant and convinced of his ability and there was always an enthusiastic and collective shout of "YES!" Then he would ask who would like to go first.

Nothing but silence. No takers.

Apparently, the audience didn't doubt *his* ability to walk

and keep his balance. He had already proven that. What they doubted was their own ability to do their part in the midst of uncertainty and fear of falling.

Throughout my life, I have never doubted that God was real and loving and looking out for me. But I *have* doubted my own ability to live into God's desire for me. I have doubted my ability to keep up my end of the deal. I have doubted, I have wavered, I have been uncertain. And in the times when I *thought* I was doubting God, it was really about me projecting my own doubt onto God.

Maybe it's the same for you or maybe it's different; that's a question only you can answer for yourself. But I do know that most of us don't come to church because we have unwavering faith and have it all figured out. Most of us are, at times, unsure of ourselves. And yet we come, because in the midst of our humanness, we need Jesus to stand in front of us, like he stood in front of Thomas that day in the upper room, confirming his resurrection. We need to know that God is still God and we are loved just the way we are, even in our feeble and sputtering faith.

Could it have been that way for Thomas? Maybe he also doubted his own ability to stay the course of faith in the face of all of the fear, the confusion, and the uncertainty about what would come next. After all, it was a lot to take in. Who's to say we wouldn't waver a little – or a lot – under the same circumstances? I have certainly faltered under much less. But we can be encouraged by Jesus' gentle handling of Thomas. He doesn't scold him for his lack of faith, or ridicule or diminish him in any way. Jesus gives Thomas the proof he needs, and therefore draws him deeper into the mystery of God. And in the midst of our own uncertainty and confusion, he does the same for us, every time. I love that about Jesus.

When it comes to our faith, it's sometimes hard to talk

about doubt. After all, what would people think? It's even harder to talk about actually doubting the events of God. In Thomas' case, it was his doubt about whether Jesus had been raised from the dead. And he wasn't alone; the Sadducees of the time taught that there was no such thing as resurrection. And the ending of Matthew's Gospel tells of how when the disciples went to meet Jesus in Galilee, that *"When they saw him, they worshipped him; but some doubted."*

We live in a culture where the western mindset all too often informs what we believe or don't believe. The analytical mind wants concrete tangible truth. Like Thomas, many of us need to see things for ourselves. We need to stick our fingers in the holes before we will believe. We need things to be reasonable and rational, proven beyond a doubt. And that's unfortunate.

Two hallmarks of our Christian faith are first the incarnation – that God came to us in human form in the person of Jesus, which means that the reality of God dwells in you and in me and in every human person – and secondly, that Jesus was resurrected from the dead into the promise of eternal life and we are given that same promise. Do you believe that, or do you doubt?

There's a lot riding on how you answer that question. If you truly believe in the incarnation – that God dwells in all people – it should change the way you live your life. And if you truly believe that God raised Jesus from the dead into eternal life and we are heirs to that eternal life, that too should change how you live your life.

Have you doubted your faith?

How did you get through it, and what did you learn?

The Audacity of Faith

MARK 5:21-43

This Gospel account from Mark finds the ministry of Jesus in full swing, and we are thrust into the midst of it all. People are buzzing about the things they have heard about Jesus. There are reports of demonic exorcisms and miraculous healings. Is it true that even the stormy Sea of Galilee became calm at his command? One report said that he had touched a leper and healed him. Can you imagine the scandal? In some cases, entire villages gathered to see him, hear his preaching, and be healed. In Capernaum, he was said to have healed a paralyzed man, and that so many were gathered around him that the man's friends had to lower his stretcher through the roof!

In the middle of all this excitement, Jairus, one of the leaders of the synagogue, has requested that Jesus come to his house. His daughter is sick, possibly dying. He needs a healer, and he needs one fast, so he calls on Jesus. It's an interesting choice coming from a prominent figure within the religious institution that has begun to grow increasingly nervous by the groundswell of support for this troublemaker from Nazareth. Then again, maybe it is the *only* choice. Jairus seems to know something, and there is no time for petty church politics. His daughter's life hangs in the balance, and he seems to know that Jesus is the man for the hour.

Jesus goes with him, but going anywhere with Jesus is not easy these days. This itinerant country preacher has drawn a crowd that seems to follow him wherever he goes, and today is no different. The crowd is pressing in on him and he himself is carried along the road in the moving sea of humanity. And then, it happens.

The text says that he was *"immediately aware that power had gone forth from him."* Whoever had reached out had actually drawn power from him. Jesus swings around and finds himself face-to-face with a woman. The woman (unnamed in the text) has fallen down before Jesus in fear and trembling because she too knows something about Jesus. This was no casual touch. This was an intentional reaching out in a faith so authentic and so affecting that it actually initiated a transmission of spiritual power. What makes it even more startling is that it was the woman who initiated it. It was *her* touching *him* – not the other way around as it had so often been before.

Just as *immediately* Jesus felt his power flow from him, so the woman was *immediately* aware that she had been healed. It was divine energy transmitting healing power from The Source to the afflicted. It was powerful yet intimate. And now the woman is before Jesus, face down and trembling, speaking a truth she knows about what just happened. The throng of onlookers is stunned. How dare she?

How dare she, a woman unclean and rejected? A woman banished to the margins of society, a woman stained by her own blood, a woman whom no one was to touch lest they themselves become unclean, having the nerve to not only reach out and touch Jesus, but to actually *take* what she needed from him? *How dare she?*

The audacity of such faith.

The woman, regardless of all outward appearances to the contrary, is not all that different from Jairus. Sure, Jairus moves in different social circles, being a leader in the synagogue. And he certainly enjoyed access to privilege that was not available to an outcast woman deemed unclean. He was respected, she was degraded; he was accepted, she was rejected.

But on this day, they are not so different. On this day they both know something. On this day, the common ground on which they find themselves is that of faith that Jesus could pull them out of trouble, that he could save the life of a twelve-year-old child and that he could heal the life of the woman who for those same twelve years had not only suffered physically, but at the not-so-clean hands of society.

And on this day, she does not let this opportunity pass her by. She does not allow herself to be left alone at the side of the road unnoticed and forgotten. She refuses to let Jesus and those pressing towards Jairus' house to do so untouched. *"If I but touch his clothes, I will be made well."* So bold. So sure. In that holy moment, time seems to stand still. In that divine connection, Jesus is one with the woman and one with the suffering. The two stand in solidarity: the woman in faith, and Jesus in love.

When the woman's reach spanned the few feet bridging the gap between herself and Jesus, it was as if she reached through Jesus to a power beyond even the miracle-worker from Nazareth to the Source of all healing; the

Source of all love, and the Source of all that is. When the woman touched the Divine Son and drew the power of God through him to her, she leveled the playing field and proved that all people have equal access to God.

The audacity of it all.

Today the woman with such audacious faith reminds us that the Good News of God in Christ is for all people. Whether we are wealthy and well-established or poor and living on the precarious, slippery edges of society, *all of us* have equal access to God's grace. Today we are reminded that whether we are black or white, rich or poor, gay or straight, we stand before God as one people, knowing that God's love is for all.

This story of the encounter with the nameless woman reminds that our faith will sometimes require making bold moves – reaching across the divide and putting ourselves on the line not just for ourselves, but for others as well. Sometimes it means that we, like the woman on that dusty road, fall down before God in fear and trembling, knowing that it is not just the only thing to do, but the *right* thing, regardless of what the crowd around us may think or say. We do it because we know something about ourselves and we know something about God. Because of that, we are able to reach out and claim what we need.

This story reminds us that no matter who we are, what we have done or failed to do, no matter where we are from or where we have been, all people are equally invited to reach out and draw what we need from God. But we must reach out. We must take the risk. How dare we, but how dare we not.

Our bold faith, being welcomed by God's amazing grace and enduring love.

The audacity of it all.

The Audacity of Faith

The holy One
within reach
of one
out of touch
pushed to the edge
unclean
who am I
to reach out
to take what I need
but I must
I must
for I know
he is the One
this is our moment
twelve years
now reaching out
contact
the power moves
from the One
to the one
now called daughter
I go in peace
healed
by the audacity of faith
by the audacity of love.

What do you need in your life, for which you must reach out to God?

Surrender
MARK 8:35

> For those who want to save their life will lose it, and those who lose their life for my sake, and for the sake of the gospel, will save it.

In western culture, largely driven by success, accomplishment, and finishing first, the idea of surrender gets a bad rap. This mindset has conditioned us to understand surrender as weakness, as defeat. Waving the white flag means that the other side has won and that we have lost. But the nature of surrender, in the spiritual sense, is more than winning or losing. It is a path to freedom.

I have had many surrenders in my life; some were because I had been driven to my knees, and some because I fell to them. Rumi once said, *"there are many ways to kneel down and kiss the ground."* Each time I have knelt down and surrendered to Truth, it has led to freedom.

Each time meant that I was letting go of something that held me back in order to grab hold of something new.

In recovery we learn that it is only through admitting utter defeat at the hands of addiction, and then dismantling our self-delusion and crushing our egos, that we are able to make a start into a better, sober, and sane life.

In 1998, I reached the bottom of my own addiction. I did not arrive willingly. It came only after decades of self-centeredness, and in later years, losing myself completely to the point of near death and insanity. It felt like I had given in to the darkness of addiction and was just waiting for the final death blow. But then, something happened. I call it Divine intervention — the loving arm of God catching me during the fall. In the end, it came with a quiet sigh of relief. Now, years later, I still wake up each day and surrender to the truth that I am powerless over my addictions and thank God for another day of sobriety. It is, as John Denver once wrote, a "sweet surrender."

In 2010, Sr. Greta and I made our monastic vows. This time I found myself on my knees before God, willingly and guided by the loving hands of fellow monks who knew about this point of surrender – about offering your heart to God. I will never forget that moment. I remember the gentle, loving touch of these wise monks as they draped the scapular over my shoulders with such care, and fussed with the hood to make sure it was just right. And it was right. This was what surrender should feel like.

We were not only giving ourselves individually to God, but also beginning our Community of Divine Love in that moment. There was a strong sense that God was starting something new, and it felt important to be a part of it. Since that day, many others have associated themselves with the community, all of them surrendering in their own way to a greater love.

Each day since has been a surrender to God's will in my life. There have been starts and stops. Sometimes my ego pokes its head in the door, just to see if I want to go on a little trip. Then I remember what a beloved friend and mentor who died with fifty-two years in recovery once said: *"Your ego is not your amigo."* Truer words were never spoken. Each time I decline the invitation for an ego-trip, I get a further glimpse of the freedom that comes only with surrendering my will over to the care of God.

When one does not know the value of surrender in their life, it can result in an ego-driven life, albeit stuck in reverse and moving away from the Divine guidance that wants only our freedom. It is a tragic thing to deny ourselves the gifts that come with the surrendered life because of our need to control and manipulate our own experience. I know this sounds counter-cultural to so many caught up in the achieving, striving, success-oriented mindset that we inherit, but ultimately it is only through surrender that we truly win at life.

What does "losing your life to gain it" mean for you?

Worthy

For many who have traveled the hard road of addiction, the journey begins at a young age under the influence of parents or adults who were lost in their own struggle, and inevitably, intentionally or not, modeled the same for the young around them. Many of these role models are well-meaning folks who care for their children. But try as we might to mask it, the outward manifestation of addiction will always show its face in subtle or not-so-subtle ways. Children are highly tuned to the ether of addiction that hangs in the air.

After years of breathing in these toxic fumes as young-sters, it becomes all too normal. The insidious idea that this is our own destiny begins to creep in. Like in the story of the frog in a pot of water, who continues to acclimate itself to the rising temperature until it boils to death, we realize too late that the waters of addiction begin to boil over into our lives. At some point along the way, we lose sight of the fact that we were worthy of a life free of addiction.

Along the way, people and opportunities may come our way: a bright, lovely romantic interest who sees beneath the tarp of addiction enough to see our truer self; a short-lived employer who recognizes potential, only to have it dashed against the rocks of our addiction; a friend who begs us to accept help. And each time, we have to turn and walk away. Each time, the lie of our unworthiness at the foundation of our addiction wins the day.

I have been around the rooms of recovery for a very long time. One of the most disappointing experiences is when some crusty long-timer turns to a new person in recovery and says something like "I hope your ass is kicked now," or "Take the cotton out of your ears and put it in your mouth," suggesting that the new person in recovery has nothing to say that is of value.

To our new friends in recovery, I say that if you hear these or similar comments, turn and walk away. This is not the language or the spirit of true recovery. All these insensitive remarks further reinforce our sense of unworthiness, increasing the risk of new people leaving to where, outside the protective canopy of a recovery community, death lurks. We should be careful with our words, because for the addict teetering on the edge, our words can bring life or death.

By the time most of us make it to recovery, we have already done a pretty good job of beating up on ourselves and filling our own heads with negative self-talk; We do not need anyone to stoke that fire further. What we *need* is water to douse the flame of self-degradation and unworthiness. What we need is love – a love that we have sought all along the way.

One of the most common characteristics of many people coming into recovery – whether they come from Wall

Street or the back alleys of life – is *shame*. It is also one of the least talked about. There is a difference between *guilt* and *shame*. Guilt is when we feel we have done something wrong. Shame is when we feel there is something wrong with us. Shame is the furnace that fuels unworthiness. Unworthiness can lead to self-loathing and a sense of defeat in life. This relationship between shame and unworthiness is evident in all the many addictive processes, which are in no way limited to alcoholism or other substance abuse. Addiction can manifest in all sorts of ways, including sex, self-harm, relationship with food, gambling, and pornography, as well as things like anger, control, and violence.

Our business in recovery, after establishing a date of sobriety, is the long, difficult, yet gentle work of restoring our sense of dignity and self-worth. It begins with naming shame. If we have the good fortune to meet someone along the way that will respectfully and lovingly guide us back to ourselves as created by God and equally beloved by God, then we have found a real treasure, one that can truly revolutionize how we see ourselves and the world around us. When we can reclaim our own worth, then we will see the worthiness in those around us, even if it is clouded by the veil of lies that once covered us. Then we can undertake the profound spiritual act of reaching out our hand and saying: "Welcome; I know how you feel."

What stands out most for you in this reflection?

Justice, Mercy, and Compassion

A Call to Truth and Reform
in the Criminal Justice System

Justice, mercy, and compassion. These are values that most all spiritual traditions strive for. In Christianity, they are the guiding principles modeled for us by Jesus, values that can be the framework of a just and healthy society. In America, however, we have a long way to go to accomplish these ideals.

Sadly, this spirit of a more compassionate society is all too often met with more than mild resistance from a criminal justice system that at times seems to be outright opposed to these principles. It seems that we have created a system that all too often prefers discrimination over justice; revenge over mercy; and punishment over compassion. Our jails and prisons bulge at the seams and lack a spirit of restoration and desire to move people into healing and wholeness.

As Angela Davis once said, our jails and prisons are filled with our social failings. Not much has changed in the nearly fifty years since she first spoke those words. Because we either lack the ability or the willingness to properly deal with issues such as racism, poverty, addiction, education, mental illness, homelessness, and violence, we try to hide our social ills from sight by throwing people in prison. However, hiding problems does not make them go away. In the meantime, people who need and deserve our help are instead tossed aside. Add to this a layer of discrimination, racism, and corrupt politics and we have a criminal justice system that is far from one that models equal justice. What we have created instead is a prison industrial complex of mass incarceration and extreme punishment. It is a system that, instead of presuming innocence as called for in the Constitution of the United States, is in reality one that presumes guilt.

The United States has the highest incarceration rate in the entire world. Since the 1970s, incarceration in this country has swelled from 300,000 to over 2.3 million. In addition, there are roughly another six million people on probation or parole supervision. 1 in every 15 people born in 2001 are expected to go to jail or prison, and one in every three Black males born in this century is expected to be incarcerated. Hundreds of thousands of non-violent offenders are forced to spend decades in prison. We have created laws such as three-strikes, where committing a minor offense like shoplifting can put people away for 25 years to life.

We have fueled the growth of the industrial prison complex through the mass incarceration of people of color, those ensconced in poverty, and those suffering from mental illness. We have waged war on people with substance abuse problems. Even more disturbing is the privatization of incarceration as a for-profit business venture. All this points to a country that, to a large degree, has abandoned the concept of truly rehabilitating people in favor of mass incarceration.

Hovering over all of this is the enormous issue of the death penalty, that stands as the ultimate example of a criminal justice system that is too often vengeful, cruel, and brutally violent. It could, and should, be argued that even people who are guilty should not be put to death, but even now, innocent people sit on the death rows of American prisons who will die unless we bring an end to the deplorable and shameful practice of these state-sanctioned revenge killings. Where is our moral, ethical, and spiritual compass? Where is the compassionate heartbeat of humanity?

What can we do? Who will come to the aid of our brothers and sisters who are treated as dispensable? If not us, then who? We must keep the conversation out front and not let those who carry out the injustices of violence and death hide under the cover of their own darkness. We must be bold enough to call out this systemic problem for what it is: racism and bigotry within the American caste system of social control.

The answer is not to build more jails and prisons. The answer is to pour our efforts into legislation that will bring about sentencing reform, and do away with things like solitary confinement, life sentences for youth, and condemning people to death. We need to stand up and shout out that there are no throwaway people. We need to pour our efforts and our money into programs and services that truly help to restore a person to the fabric of community and the love of God. This is the work of the reign of God's justice here on earth. Yes, we have a long way to go, but it begins with each of us right now.

Come to Me

MATTHEW 11:28-30

This invitation from Jesus is about struggle and relief; it is about despair and hope; it is about finding a way to share the sometimes-crushing load of life.

When a young ox is being trained to pull heavy loads, it is first yoked with a stronger, mature ox at its side. The young ox has the yoke over its shoulders just as the older one does and makes all the movements, but does little, if any, of the actual pulling. It is the older, stronger ox that pulls the load, with the younger one at its side keeping stride. Eventually, as the younger ox gains strength and learns technique, it begins to shoulder some of the weight until eventually it pulls an equal load. Someday it too will train a younger ox, and so it goes.

The metaphor of yoking is what Jesus uses to describe his invitation to bring him our burdens. He is saying "whatever it is that is bothering you, whatever it is that is just too much for you to bear; whatever it is that seems impossible to find your way through; bring it to me, let me have it, I can take it. It is not too heavy for me, for you are my beloved. You are my sister or brother."

"Come to me, all of you who are weary and carrying heavy burdens, and I will give you rest."

Jesus also says that he will teach us in his gentleness and says that in his humility, we will find rest for our weary souls. When we have run out of answers for our lives, when we have nowhere and no one to turn to, Jesus says "Come to me". When we are bruised and beaten, when we are about to give up because the weight is too much and we can't take one more step, Jesus steps in. He lifts our burden: the burden of sadness, the burden of oppression, the burden of addiction, the burden of violence, the burden of victimhood, the burden of loneliness.

This is a hard world that we live in, one that can sometimes be cruel and cold. It is a world that offers us so many temptations that lead to destruction. But it is also a world that God so loved that he sent his Son. And God so loves you.

Jesus invites us to take up his yoke and let him carry our burdens. He does not demand that we make the choice, but he hopes that we will. And his heart must sink when we choose another way.

This divine invitation is also a reminder to us that we too can help others shoulder their burdens. Just as Jesus offers himself to us as a source of strength and a way to ease our burdens, we too can offer ourselves to one another. When we have a brother or sister who is struggling under the weight of life, we can help to ease the pain, to ease the burden. When we see another lost in loneliness, we are called into community with that person. When we see another heartbroken with sadness, we can offer loving kindness. When we see another lost in the dark night of the soul, we can be a window to the sunlight of the spirit.

We are all called to be instruments of peace, kindness, justice, and love for one another. We should not listen to the voice of deception that says we are enemies. That voice leads only to conflict, violence and heartache.

We know the truth that speaks to our hearts. There is no denying the still, soft voice of God within that encourages us to be in kinship with one another. I know that you hear it and I pray that you will listen. It is the voice of God that directs us to peace and hopes for our freedom.

Come to our brother Jesus, those of us who are heavy with burdens and we will find rest. Take his yoke upon us and let him teach us, because he is humble and gentle, and we will find a place to rest. For his yoke fits perfectly and the burden he gives us is light.

What is it that you struggle with most?

What keeps you from truly handing it over to God?

Greater Love

tears of joy and sadness
oh, the sacrifices we make
for greater Love

This poem reflects on the nature of the sweet surrender of finite loves – be they material or human – that are sacrificed for the greater Divine Love of God. It speaks to the bittersweet truth that authenticity of our relationship with the Divine Reality comes at a cost, and yet fosters a deep abiding joy.

I have had moments in my life when I realized that some of the things I had been striving for, thinking that they would fill the longing within me, needed to be released so I could be free to experience the greater love of God. When I was able to let go and trust God, I was set on a path to experience real authentic love that I had never dreamed possible. I learned that the longing for God can only be filled by the things of God. When I was able to give myself fully to the Divine Love that gave itself fully to me, I learned what true love really is.

Bent Over

LUKE 13:10-17

The synagogue is teeming with those who have come from near and far on this Sabbath Day to worship God, coming from all walks of life – rich and poor, old and young, common people and religious elite alike. Quietly moving through the crowd, unnoticed, is a woman bent over with her head down. She has been crippled for eighteen years. It's not easy for her to make the trip to the synagogue. It's a struggle, and yet she comes, week after week, to praise God. There is nothing in the text to indicate she is asking for anything; not mercy, not pity, not even healing. She simply comes to worship God.

Imagine, if you can, what it must have been like for her. Eighteen years of feeling the weight pushing down on her. Eighteen years of looking at the ground. Eighteen years of not being able to turn her face to the sun. Eighteen years of pain. And still, she comes to praise God.

Amid the crowd and the noise, she hears the voice of the poor one from Nazareth. Is this the one she has heard about? Will he preach today? But instead, he turns his attention to her. The one with gentle eyes and worker hands reaches out – with a word, a touch, with love – and just like that, she is healed. It is a stunning scene. Nothing else is needed. The sermon that some may have come to hear has come to life before their eyes. Those gathered buzz with excitement. They have seen a miracle.

The woman looks up. She can see the stunned faces. As she looks into the eyes of Jesus, she sees love. As she looks into the eyes of the Pharisees, she sees rage.

The text says that the leader of the synagogue was indignant because Jesus had healed on the Sabbath. Jesus would have none of it. This is not the first time that he called out the religious leaders as hypocrites, and it would not be the last. Imagine how it was that day in the synagogue, as their arrogant annoyance with Jesus turned to shame, with the crowd roaring its approval and rejoicing at all the wonderful things he was doing. This itinerant rabbi, a country preacher from a backwater town, was once again stirring things up and turning things upside down.

There is a lot at play in this scene, and it all centers on the moment between Jesus and this unnamed woman – a woman who was bent over under the oppression of not only her physical condition but also of the societal pressures around her. The leader of the synagogue was also bent over under the weight of his own short-sightedness, narrow-mindedness, and disregard for the suffering of those around him. We all need liberation – some from oppression, and others from privilege.

Mother Teresa once said that most all our problems today are because we have forgotten that we belong to one another. I think the problem that the leader of the synagogue was faced with is that he thought that the woman was somehow separated from him and his life. That he was unaffected and therefore uninterested. Even worse, he was all too willing to let the rigid structure of the church get in the way of doing God's work. Clearly, he saw the woman as the "other." But there is no "other;" there is only "us." To see things any other way is an illusion. Ravi Shankar once said that the spiritual journey in life is one of becoming somebody, to becoming nobody, to becoming everybody.

Many of us have our own version of being bent over by the struggle of life. Maybe it is an economic crisis, an addiction, a threatening diagnosis, or a troubled relationship. We all have been, or will be, faced with struggle. Many people are bent under the weight of continually having to accommodate themselves to a society that considers them different or less valuable than others. It is a society built on caste that makes assumptions about people who appear different from the majority group or the privileged group or the dominant caste. The result is that people are bent under the burden of racism, sexism, economic inequality, cultural or religious bias, ableism, and numerous other forces of oppression.

In our life with our incarcerated friends, we are engaged with many who are bent over. The oppression that pushes down on them is that of racism, bigotry, poverty, drug addiction/alcoholism, mental illness, homelessness, unemployment and lack of equal educational opportunity. They are victims of a system of society that would rather hide these social ills in our jails and prisons than do the hard work of helping them in the ways that they need. Incarceration has all too often become the response of first resort for dealing with the issues that plague our society. The problem with this approach is that the things that we are trying to hide do not go away. All that disappears is the human being. Whether we know it or not, our society groans under the weight of such shameful practices. We are bent over by a system of oppression that we ourselves have created.

The story of Jesus healing the woman is at minimum a call for a little humility on our part. When we posture ourselves in the way of humility and kinship with others, good things can happen. I have heard it said a thousand different ways by those we sit with in jails and prisons: they feel that they have never had someone really listen to them. They have not had someone interested enough to learn about who they are, or value what they say. The truth is that we all have a lot to say, and to dismiss people for any reason is to miss the gift they bring.

That day in the synagogue, when the bent-over woman was invisible to many, Jesus noticed her and made the first move. We are here to *notice* one another and to mirror the truth for each other that we are all beloved by God and important to the divine enterprise that is God's work here on earth. We are here to return our True Selves to each other as the *Imago Dei* – the image of God – in which we were all created. We are here to remind each other that we are nothing less than the absolute apple of God's eye, as bent-over as we may be.

Anything else is an illusion.

Like Mary, Like Judas

JOHN 12:1-8

This story from the Gospel according to John is set in an interesting place with an interesting cast of characters. Lazarus is there along with Mary, Martha and Judas. The story doesn't tell us why they are gathered, only that they gave a dinner for Jesus.

It would make sense that the first three would throw a dinner party for Jesus out of their gratitude for raising Lazarus from the dead, but what about the fifth guest? What about Judas? It is rather peculiar to me that he is invited into this scene, only because there is no indication that any of the other disciples are there. So why Judas?

Putting that question aside for a moment. this prelude to the Passion is a beautiful domestic scene where Jesus seems to have experienced as close to the feeling of "home" as ever since his ministry began. Lazarus, Martha and Mary are his intimate friends, and now they gather with him at an important time.

This also feels like an intimate act of love from a devoted disciple toward her beloved Lord. In this scene, Mary serves as the perfect model for Christian discipleship. The act of anointing the feet of Jesus with oil is as extravagant as it is humble. Like John, Mary is a dedicated witness and a disciple, not just by what she says but by what she does. She quietly, powerfully, and lovingly goes about her duty.

This story is notable because it illustrates that Jesus' journey to the cross includes not only Mary, a faithful disciple who pours out her love at his feet, but also Judas, the unfaithful disciple who steals from the common purse and will ultimately betray Jesus. Both play an important role, and their inclusion tells us something about the all-encompassing nature of God's grace. It also poses some difficult questions.

Jesus said that he came not for the righteous, but also for the sinner. The shepherd claims that he would leave the flock of ninety-nine to save just one. If there was ever one who was lost, it is Judas, the one who would betray Jesus. This is a message of great hope for humankind and one that says that no one is beyond the grace and love of God. The fact is that Judas is no less a witness and a disciple than Mary, and he is no less loved by God than Mary or anyone else. And that is very good news for the rest of us.

It is so much easier for us to align ourselves with Mary and her loving devotion than it is to relate ourselves to Judas and our own potential for unfaithfulness and betrayal. It is natural for us to want to be like Mary, devoted to the end and extravagant in our outpouring of love. It's harder for us to watch as Judas succumbs to the seduction of greed, or to hear about when Peter denies knowing Jesus because he fears losing the very life he once boldly claimed he would give for his closest friend. Maybe it's harder because the disciples are in many ways composites of ourselves; the good and the not so good, the faithful and the not so faithful. We want to be like Mary, not Judas. It's easy for us to see the Mary in ourselves, but not so easy to look at the Judas staring back at us in the mirror. The truth is, we are all like Mary, or at least we can be. The same is true for our propensity to be like Judas.

Reflecting on this scripture brings with it both the opportunity to embrace the Mary within us as we move deeper into prayer and devotion. We also have the challenge of exposing the shadowy corners of the unfaithfulness of Judas within ourselves.

It's not easy to give ourselves to deep searching and self-examination, It is challenging work, but work that can bear much fruit. Getting in touch with the shadow side of ourselves that might be less than what we would admit to the world – or even to ourselves – is the very thing that can free us to be the faithful and devoted disciples that we want to be and who God wants us to be.

Sometimes the truth about ourselves is hard to swallow. Nonetheless, it is a process that is necessary if we want to free ourselves to be more like Mary. We must get in touch with the other part of us that is in the room, the one that objects for selfish reasons, the one that is tempted into betrayal. It is when we can name the Judas within us that we grow into our True Self.

We need not sit in sorrow like Judas wishing that we could give back the things that have sold us out. We can see the example set for us by the contrasting models of discipleship of Mary and Judas, and claim who we want to be. We can move away from selfish and self-serving ways and move into a loving and generous way of being, and that is good enough. God does not ask that we be perfect, only that we be faithful.

So why is Judas invited into this party scene in this story? It might be because there is more than one way for God to make the point with us. We learn much about who we want to be by observing the example of Mary. We also learn much about who we do not want to be by observing the example of Judas. Both carry important messages about discipleship.

All of us are about so much more than the little ways of Judas. The invitation is to repent and leave those ways behind, and sit at the feet of our Teacher in devotion, anointing with the perfume which fills the room with our love and faithfulness. It is then that we can sit at the foot of the cross and caress Jesus in his suffering. It is then that we are free to live like Lazarus, raised from the death of our own darkness into the resurrected life of Jesus Christ. It is the great Christian hope that is seen as we sit, like Mary, at the feet of our Lord, free to love, free to die, and free to rise again.

How are you like Mary?

How are you like Judas?

Love Notes

"My religion is love." This phrase has been quoted by so many people, it is impossible to credit them all. I often insert it into the hundreds of letters I write to my friends living behind the wall each year. It rings with universal truth, and like most profound things, it is simple in nature.

The idea that love is what holds the center of one's spiritual life is commonly held. It also cuts through some of the dogma that can often bog people down. Who could argue against such a pure and clear understanding of what religion can be at its best?

As a follower of Jesus, I look to his teachings and the life he modeled for us. What I hear and see from him is love, and from that, all sorts of spiritual grace can flow through us and flood into the world.

Was Jesus a prophet? Yes. Was he an advocate for justice and truth? Certainly. Was he a divine human pathway to God? No doubt. He was and is all these things, and at his core he was love – love for people and love for God. It was his love that fueled his actions. It was love that allowed him to heal others and see people in a way that they had never been seen before. Look through all the stories, the parables, and the encounters that comprise the narrative of his life. Love is the golden thread that runs through it all, from his arrival in a cattle stall to his ultimate statement of love in his last gasping breath on earth from the cross.

Love is also the language of perennial wisdom of the mystics, poets, saints, and sages of all traditions throughout the ages. Mahatma Gandhi once said that he considered himself a Hindu, Christian, Muslim, Jew, Buddhist, and Confucian. He went on to join the many who claim love as their religion. Can you see the beauty in this universal truth? Can you see how it is love that binds us together yet transcends religious structures and institutions?

I wasn't always able to.

Like with many others, the examples that were modeled for me growing up in a family system riddled with alcoholism, violence and abuse were distorted and dysfunctional. Family members were closed off emotionally, walking on eggshells in fear and distrust. It was not a family culture that was conducive to nurturing and care. All of us need a sense that we are loved, and we also need to be able to express love. These are basic human instincts.

But what was it like for someone like me, who had no real idea of what true love looked and felt like? By sheer grace, as a young person I sensed God's care and love. I was most aware of it when I was in solitude. That quiet awareness is what got me through. It felt like a cherished secret between God and me. When it came to fostering and nurturing loving relationships with people, however, I didn't know where to begin. In my early years of adulthood, I had many opportunities from lovely women come my way. Unfortunately, I didn't have the healthy imprint which others seemed to have, nor did I have the skill set, so I fumbled my way through. I looked for love in dysfunctional ways. I became extremely clingy to anyone who showed me affection, which is understandable for someone who, underneath all the facades, was starving for it. Then things changed.

My first attempt at sobriety came in 1986. Although I was not able to maintain my recovery beyond a few years, I was introduced to people who worked on issues like my own "love wound." The seed had been planted. It would be several years before I would be able to achieve permanent sobriety and recovery, essential grounding for someone like me. Now I have now been in continuous recovery since early 1998. The work of my recovery program and the spiritual pursuit of my true self has flung the doors of my heart open, and the flood of love has real, true meaning in my life. What I have found is that my "love secret" with God all those years ago was the seed that since has sprouted into continuous bloom. The love that I share with others now is healthy and authentic because the model I try my best to follow is healthy and authentic. It is from God, Jesus, and all my friends who practice real love and help guide my way.

When it comes down to it, all of the essays in this book are love notes – from one person to another, from God to us, and from us to God. In the end, it all boils down to love. When I come to the end of my life, I will not be judged by how successful or accomplished I was, but by how I loved or failed to love.

Some years ago, Anna, an Episcopal priest and one of our volunteers in the jails, had a young woman approach her after a class she taught at CRDF, the women's jail in Lynwood, California. The young woman explained that she had heard Anna talk about the Episcopal Church, in terms of its spirit and commitment to full inclusion of all people including the LGBTQ community, and wondered if it could be true. Our priest explained that she was proud to be a member of a church that knew that all people were created in God's divine image and equally loved by God. Tears welled up in the young woman's eyes and she said, "Are you telling me that as a gay woman, I can be a Christian? Because no one else is telling me that." Anna told her that not only could she be a Christian, but that she was beautiful and beloved by God.

This was church community at its best. This is what it means to be a community of Jesus led by the Spirit of love.

He Asked For Charity

God came to my house and asked for charity.
And I fell on my knees and
Cried, "Beloved.

what may I
give?"

"Just love," He said.
"Just love."

-Francis of Assisi

In Gratitude

I am grateful for so many who have helped this book become a reality. First, for my monastic community writers, Sister Greta and Brother Mitch, who listened to these words for countless hours in our writer's group meetings. You offered me wisdom and honesty about the writing as only other writers can. You inspire me to be better, and your fingerprints are on these pages. For my editor, Alysha Kawamoto, not only for your editing skills, but for your willingness to have the conversations that make this a better book. For Carrie Voris, for your amazing graphic design work, editing, and bringing this book across the finish line to print. Your professionalism, patience, creativity and friendship are invaluable. For my dear friend and recovery guide, Don Maxwell, who cheers me on like a father would a son. I can only hope that you are proud of the work of life that we have created together. Lastly, for all my friends living behind the walls of incarceration. You have taught me so much about dignity, truth, resiliency, sisterhood/brotherhood, and love. This book is for you.

For more information about our
Community of Divine Love
visit www.cdlmonks.org.

Made in the USA
Las Vegas, NV
15 September 2022

55365792R00075